Helpful Hints:

Always lay your work on a flat surface to get a true measurement.

Backing up beads on the thread means you should push the beads further back on the thread towards the spool.

Read through each project first to become familiar with it. Then, gather all your supplies.

Practice a Chain Stitch with the thread and beads for a couple of inches. This will help you become familiar with the thread and give you more control over the tension. Pull out the practice stitches before you start.

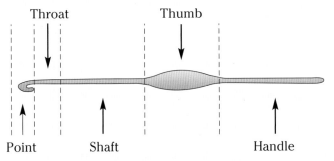

Anatomy of a Crochet Hook

Holding your Hook

Grasp the hook by the thumb rest using your middle finger or index finger, whichever feels more comfortable. Gently hold the handle in the palm of your hand.

Hold the hook towards your heart. All you need is a slight downward motion to pick up your thread. Holding the hook underhanded has been shown to cause less stress on your wrist.

Some projects take a while to complete and being comfortable is important.

Holding the thread in your left hand, gently grasp the thread with your middle, ring, and pinky fingers. Bring the working thread up between the middle finger and across the index finger.

Once the cord has been started, hold the cord between your index finger and thumb and pull the next bead down with the index finger of your other hand. Slide the hook across your finger, picking up the thread on the other side of the bead, with work off the loops.

If you are left-handed, follow the directions working from the right instead of the left.

More information on crochet is available on the craft yarn council website at www.learntocrochet.com.

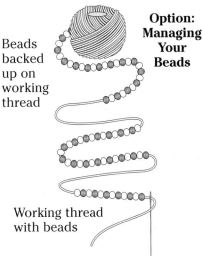

Option: Managing Your Beads

Beads backed up on working thread

Working thread with beads

Threading the Beads:

You will be threading beads onto your crochet thread. To do this, use a #10 or #12 size beading needle with the Coats and Clark #69 thread.

If you find it difficult to thread the needle, try using a small loop of Nymo beading thread through the eye of the needle, then slip the larger thread through the smaller loop. This method will also work with the size #18 cord.

A #7 sharp needle will work with size #18 cord.

Stringing the Beads

You can string the beads by scooping them out of a flat dish or jar lid.

Or you can use a bead spinner tool that helps you string seed beads without having to pick them up one at a time; however, this cannot be used when you have to change bead colors to create interesting patterns.

Stringing instructions are with each project.

Storing the Threaded Beads

Use a small dish, soup bowl, or a large cup. Once the beads are on the thread, push the beads along the thread so they don't fall off the end.

Place the spool into the dish for easy storage. Work each project from the spool of thread.

In case of broken thread or should you need to join a new thread, first transfer the remaining beads to the new thread. Use the last loop to pull a loop from the new thread through, pull the old loop tight. Knot the two threads together, keeping the hook in the new loop, so you won't lose it.

Continue the crochet leaving the knot in the center of your work. This will join the work seamlessly.

continued on page 16

Blue Candy Combo
pages 8 - 9

**Indonesian Bead
Necklace**
pages 10 - 11

**Floral Charm
Bracelet**
page 12

Necklace with Spiral
pages 12 - 13

Aboriginal Basic Lariat
page 19

Green Spiral Necklace
pages 20 - 21

Earring Necklaces
pages 22 - 23

Lime Green Necklace
page 28

**Stars & Stripes
Necklace**
page 30

**Stars & Stripes
Bangles**
page 31

Bangles
page 32

Index of Projects

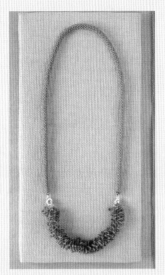

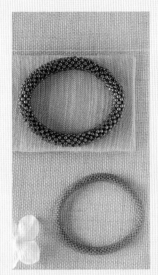

'Change A Bead' Necklace
pages 14 - 15

Memory Wire Bracelet
page 17

Pink Candy Combo
pages 16 - 17

Blue & Pink Bangles
page 18

Create a Loop Lariat
pages 24 - 25

Confetti Bangle Bracelet
page 26

Confetti Multi-Strand Necklace
page 27

Chunky Necklace
page 33

Mixed Size Bead Bracelet
page 34

Mixed Size Bead Necklace
page 35

continued from page 3

Reading the Pattern

Backing up beads on the thread means pushing the beads further back on the thread towards the spool. Read through each project first, becoming familiar with it.

Gather your supplies.

Practice a Chain Stitch for a few inches. Pull this back out before you start. If the thread becomes a bit fuzzy just snip it off. Keep your sense of humor, we all have to start somewhere.

A list of supplies will start each project.

Finishing tips are included throughout each project to give them a bit of professional polish.

Practice Making a Chain

Practice making a Chain Stitch with your thread before you begin your projects.

This will help you to learn to control the tension. Controlling the tension is the key to having projects turn out right.

Never change crochet hook gauge. In bead crochet controlling the tension with the proper size hook is very important.

Practicing with the thread will give you the confidence to work these projects.

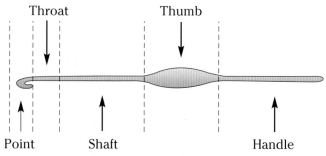

Anatomy of a Crochet Hook

Basic Bead Crochet

Following is the basic pattern for 5 in the round bead cord.

First, thread the beads for your project.

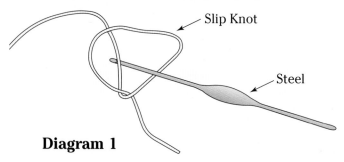

Diagram 1

Make a Slip knot (see Diagram 1), leaving an 8"-10" long tail. (Diagram 2).

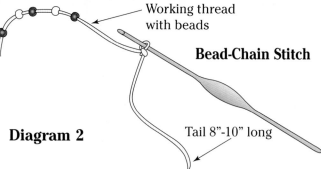

Bead-Chain Stitch

Diagram 2

With that first loop on the hook, keeping the tension slightly tight, push the first bead close to the hook. Hook the thread on the left side of the bead (Diagram 3).

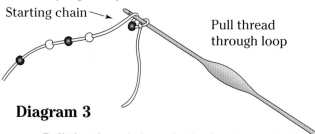

Diagram 3

Pull the thread through the first loop, leaving the bead in the middle of the loop.

Repeat this process 4 more times, for a total of 5 Chain (ch.) stitches (sts.). (Diagram 4)

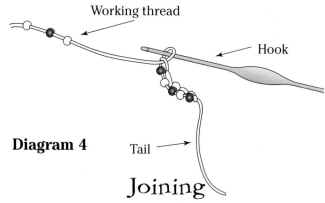

Diagram 4

Joining

To create a round, keep the last loop on the hook after you Chain 5. Turn back to the first loop in the chain, right next to the Slip knot. Turn the bead just slightly forward so you can see the stitch at the back of the bead. (Diagram 5).

This also works for 4 in the round.

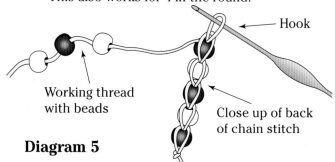

Diagram 5

Working the Round

With the hook still in the loop you just joined and holding onto the tail, give the work a very gentle tug. This should help line the work up a little better. Turn the first bead in the chain slightly back. Push the hook through the left side of the loop with the bead on it. (Diagram 5).

Push the next bead on the working thread up close to the hook and pull a new loop with bead in the middle through both loops. The bead will sit on the top of the first bead in the joined chain. Repeat this process with each bead, working in a spiral until reaching desired length. When you begin, keep the tension as even as possible, keeping the hook in the last loop worked and gently tugging the working thread. This helps even out the tension.

Keep your eye on the thread. Work the bead in the round that sits right in front of the thread, for it is always the next stitch.

If it does not look right, just pull the work back out and start over. Practicing once or twice will make a better cord. If the thread becomes a little fuzzy, just pull the work out and back up the beads. Cut off the fuzzy thread, and start again.

All but three projects in this book is based on this simple process.

Join with a Bead-Slip Stitch

Working thread must be behind and above the next stitch. Push the hook through the top thread on the left side of the knot. (Diagram 6).

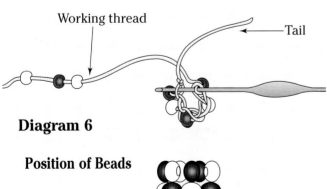

Diagram 6

Position of Beads

Beads that have not been stitched stand in a vertical position.

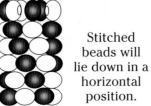

Stitched beads will lie down in a horizontal position.

Finishing

When you reach the desired length of cord, the last round can be worked by simply Slip stitching without a bead. This pulls all the beads in line.

If you are working a bangle, do not work a Slip stitch round, leave the last round undone.

Pull one last loop through. Cut the working thread 12" from the loop. Push the end of the working thread through the loop. Pull the new tail tight. You can use the tail on both ends to attach findings or beads to finish according to the project you have chosen.

Without a bead in the middle, hook the working thread and pull a new loop through both loops on the hook. (Diagram 7).

The round is now Slip stitched together.

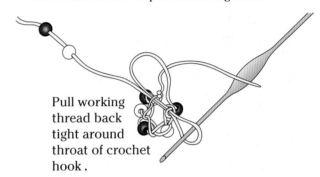

Pull working thread back tight around throat of crochet hook.

Diagram 7

Finishing

Thread the working thread onto a needle. (Diagram 8). Pass the needle through 1 bead and tie a Finishing Knot.

Run the needle back and forth through the crocheted cord several times to secure. Trim the tails.

Repeat for the other end.

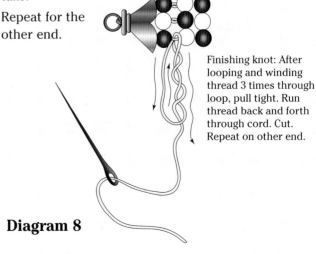

Finishing knot: After looping and winding thread 3 times through loop, pull tight. Run thread back and forth through cord. Cut. Repeat on other end.

Diagram 8

continued on page 8

continued from page 7

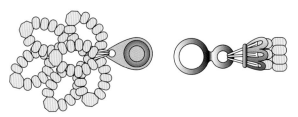

Ball and Socket Clasp

Fancy Toggle Clasp

Basic Cord Necklaces

Each of these projects are worked in the basic 5 or 4 in the round Slip stitch crochet.

To Shorten or Lengthen a Pattern

For size 11° beads, there are approximately 11 beads in an inch. 11 times 5 equals 1" of worked cord. This means that if you want a cord that is 18" long you will need 990 beads, or about 21-23 grams.

For size 8° beads, there are 8 beads per inch. 8 times 5 equals 40 beads per inch of worked cord. For 18", you need 720 beads or 21-23 grams of beads.

Tip: Always buy a little extra, in case you spill some beads. Also, the bead manufacturers try very hard to keep the colors consistent, but it is best to purchase all the beads needed for each color from the same color lot.

Tip: If you are working with a bead you are unfamiliar with, make a small test cord. Crochet 2" and then measure 1" in the middle of the test cord. That plus a little math will give you the amount of beads you'll need for your project.

Candy Combo Necklace

Here's a great example of a bracelet-necklace duo. These luminous cobalt blue beads bring a bit of adventure to your accessory wardrobe.

Blue Candy Bracelet:

This bracelet is worked only with a chain stitch.

SIZE: 7" including clasp

MATERIALS:
Conso Navy #18 nylon cord
2 tubes *Miyuki* 356c Star Sapphire 8° or 6° seed beads
77 Cobalt Blue 6 mm rondel Czech fire polish focal beads
1 *Jane's Fiber and Beads* Silver ball and socket clasp
Crochet steel hook (*Susan Bates* #4 or *Wright/Boye* #7)
#7 sharp cotton darner needle

STRING THE BEADS:
Thread onto spool: 5 seed beads, 1 focal bead, 10 seed beads, 1 focal bead. Continue with repeat of 10 seed beads and 1 focal bead until only 1 focal bead remains. Then add 5 seed beads after the last focal bead.

CONSTRUCTION:
Make a Slip knot leaving an 8"-10" tail. Count the first 5 seed beads, 1 focal bead, and 5 seed beads. Using the crochet hook, grasp thread just the other side of the last 5 seed beads. Pull new loop through the first loop, keeping the stitches very tight. This creates a loop of 5 seed beads, 1 focal bead, and 5 seed beads with each stitch.

Work all the beads on the thread into loops. Keep the tension very tight while you work. It is the natural state for this bracelet to curl around itself. When you reach the desired length, pull the last loop out about 10", cut in the middle of the loop and pull the working thread back out.

This leaves a nice neat knot and tail. Use the tail at both ends to attach the findings. You can make this bracelet shorter or longer by using this formula: 11 Chain stitches equal 1" of bracelet. Within the 11 Chain stitches, there should be 11 loops of 11 focal beads with 5 seed beads on both sides of the focal bead. This pattern will stretch just a bit.

Blue Cord for Necklace:

Make a simple cord necklace... then attach it to the Candy Bracelet to create a stunning piece

SIZE: 18" including clasp

MATERIALS:
1 spool *Conso* Navy #18 nylon cord
3 tubes *Miyuki* 356c Star Sapphire 8° seed beads
1 *Jane's Fiber and Beads* Silver ball and socket clasp
2 Silver end caps
Crochet steel hook (*Susan Bates* #4 or *Wright/Boye* #7)
#7 needle

STRING THE BEADS:
Thread the beads onto the cord.

CONSTRUCTION:
Work 5 in the round to 18". (See pages 6-7.) Finish ends, thread through end caps to attach clasps.

Use this necklace with the Blue Candy Bracelet.

Indonesian Bead Necklace

When you really love a particular bead, but you only have a few, combine them with all your other "orphan" beads to make a stunning work of art. Add texture and contrast to any outfit by using a wide variety of colors and bead sizes.

You can vary this pattern by changing the size of the focal beads. Work this necklace in the same pattern as the Candy Bracelet on page 8, using the same formula as the bracelet to create an 18" necklace. Use tails at either end to attach findings.

SIZE: 20" including clasp

MATERIALS:
Mastex Pewter #18 nylon cord
3 tubes *Miyuki* F451D Atmosphere Grey 8° or 6° seed beads
198 *Bead World* Indonesian focal beads in mixed sizes of
    11 different beads
1 *Springall Adventures* Silver clasp SRS116A/B
#4 *Susan Bates* crochet steel hook (#7 *Boye/ Wrights*)
#7 sharp cotton darner needle

STRING THE BEADS:
Thread onto spool: 5 seed beads, 1 focal bead, 10 seed beads, 1 focal bead. Continue with repeat of 10 seed beads and 1 focal bead until only 1 focal bead remains. Then add 5 seed beads after the last focal bead. Your focal beads can be placed in a pattern or completely at random.

CONSTRUCTION:
Make a Slip knot leaving an 8"-10" tail. Count the first 5 seed beads, 1 focal bead, and 5 seed beads. Using the crochet hook, hook the thread just to the other side of the last 5 seed beads. Pull this new loop through the first loop, keeping the stitches very tight. This is called a Chain stitch. It creates a loop of 5 seed beads, 1 focal bead, 5 seed beads with each stitch.

Work all the beads on the thread into loops. Keep the tension very tight while you work. It is the natural state for this bracelet to curl around itself.

When you reach the desired length, pull the last loop out about 10", cut in the middle of the loop and pull the working thread back out. This leaves a nice neat knot and tail. Use the tail at both ends to attach the findings.

You can make this bracelet shorter or longer by using this formula: 11 Chain stitches equal 1" of bracelet. Within the 11 Chain stitches, there should be 11 loops of 11 focal beads with 5 seed beads on both sides of the focal bead. This pattern will stretch just a bit.

Floral Charm Bracelet

Complement a one-of-a-kind glass bead with elegant findings and silver charms. Sparkling seed beads enhance the colors in the glass, creating a harmonious piece of jeweled art.

SIZE: 8" including clasp

MATERIALS:
1 spool *Conso* Slate #18 Nylon cord
1 tube 21-23 grams *Toho* 8R288 Light Blue 8° seed beads
1 *Diane Bentley* lampwork glass bead no larger than ½"
Jane's Fiber and Beads Marcasite Silver (1 clasp, 2 end caps, 2 beads)
1 *Springall Adventures* Silver heart charm
Crochet steel hook (*Susan Bates* #4 or *Wright/Boye* #7)
#7 sharp needle

STRING THE BEADS:
Thread the seed beads.

CONSTRUCTION:
Measure the clasp closed with the lampwork bead next to it. This should measure 2". Work 5 in the round, leaving a 10" tail, until the beaded cord measures 6". If you want a shorter or longer cord, add or subtract rounds according to your personal wrist measurement.

On one end, thread an endcap, Silver bead, lampwork bead, Silver bead, and a jump ring. Take the thread back through the beads. Push the needle into the cord and knot. Go back through the beads and jump ring again. Take the thread back through the beads into the cord and knot again.

Work the thread back and forth once or twice, then cut off close to the cord. Attach the clasp and charm to the jump ring.

Attach the endcap and clasp to the other end in the same manner.

Necklace with Spiral

Here's a gorgeous necklace with an asymmetrical twist. With sophisticated style, the shorter cord ends in an awesome lamp-work bead.

SIZE: 16" including clasp

MATERIALS:
1 spool *Mastex* Pewter #18 nylon cord
1 spool #69 *Coats & Clark* Neutral
2 *Marvin Overman* lampwork beads
1 tube each *Miyuki* (F463 Amethyst Berry 8°, F451d Atmosphere Gray 11°)
1 strand Copper Lined Clear 3 mm Czech fire polish beads
1 *Jane's Fiber and Beads* Silver ball and socket clasp
Crochet steel hooks
(*Susan Bates* #4 & #11 or
Wrights/Boye #7 & #11)
Needles (#7 sharp, #10 beading)

Basic Necklace:

STRING THE BEADS:
Mix the fire polish with the 8° seed beads in a small dish. Thread the beads in a random order onto the #18 cord.

CONSTRUCTION:
Work 4 in the round, leaving an 8"-10" tail. (See pages 6-7.) Work until you reach 17" of crochet cord.

Attach the clasp on either side using the tails.

Spiral:

You are going to make 2 pieces of 4 in the round cord, one 7½" and the other 1" long.

SIZE: 10" including lampwork beads

STRING THE BEADS:
Thread the 11° seed beads onto the Coats & Clark thread.

CONSTRUCTION:
Attach the 7½" cord 4" from the clasp to the main body of the necklace. Attach the smaller bead to the larger bead with the 1" section. Wrap the smaller cord loosely around the body of the main necklace, until the larger bead hangs in the center of the necklace.

Using the Coats & Clark threaded on the beading needle, gently tack stitch the 7½" cord to the center of the necklace.

Feel free to gently Tack stitch it in a couple of spots, just not too tightly.

Basic Cord
for a
'Change A Bead'
Necklace

Now you can wear a beautiful array of lamp-work beads as pendants on the same necklace!

The quick switch bead post allows you to easily change the pendants to match your mood or wardrobe.

SIZE: 20" including clasp

MATERIALS:
1 spool *Mastex* 770 Fern #18 cord
42-46 grams *Miyuki* F650 Parrot Green 8° seed beads
Several *Marvin Overman* lampwork beads in varying sizes
1 *Jane's Fiber and Beads* knocker Silver clasp
1 *Barley Beads* SS Quick Switch Bead Post
2 Silver tulip end caps
Crochet steel hook (*Susan Bates* #4 or *Wright/Boye* #7)
#7 needle

STRING THE BEADS:
Thread the beads.

CONSTRUCTION:
This necklace is worked 4 in the round until you reach 19".
(See pages 6-7.)

Finish ends and attach findings.

Follow manufacturer's instructions to attach the Quick Switch Bead post.

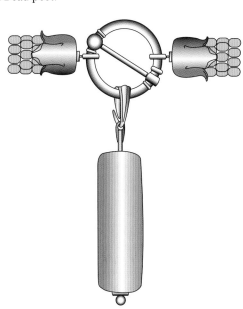

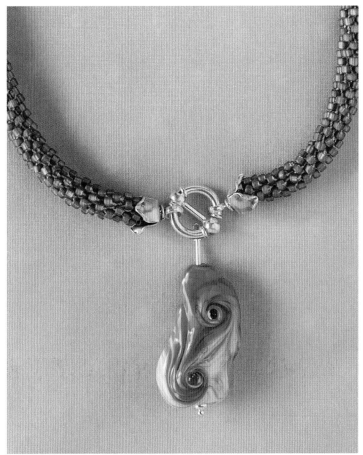

Candy Combo

Add a bit of romance to your wardrobe with a dusty rose necklace and bracelet.

Attach the bracelet to the necklace to create an elegant alternative for a spring evening.

This variance of the Blue Candy bracelet pattern uses 11° seed beads.

Pink Candy Bracelet

This bracelet is worked only with a chain stitch.

SIZE: 7" including clasp

MATERIALS:
1 spool Pink #69 *Coats and Clark* 100% nylon upholstery thread
1 tube *Miyuki* 142b Rose Grey 11° seed beads
140 Pink 3 mm Czech fire polish focal beads
1 *Jane's Fiber and Beads* Silver ball and socket clasp
Crochet steel hook (*Susan Bates* #10 or *Wright/Boye* #11)
#10 beading needle

STRING THE BEADS:
Thread onto spool: 5 seed beads, 1 focal bead, 10 seed beads, 1 focal bead. Continue with repeat of 10 seed beads and 1 focal bead until only 1 focal bead remains. Then add 5 seed beads after the last focal bead.

CONSTRUCTION:
Work this bracelet in the same pattern as the Blue Candy Bracelet on page 8. This Pretty Pink Bracelet will create a smaller loop of beads.

Use the formula of 20 stitches per inch to increase or decrease the length of the bracelet.

Pink Cord for Necklace

Make a simple cord necklace... then attach it to the Candy bracelet to create a stunning piece.

SIZE: 18" including clasp

MATERIALS:
1 spool *Coats and Clark* #69 thread
1 tube *Miyuki* 142 Rose Gray 11° seed beads
1 *Jane's Fiber and Beads* Silver ball and socket clasp
2 Silver end caps
Crochet steel (*Susan Bates* #10 or *Wright/Boye* #11)
#10 or #12 beading needle

STRING THE BEADS:
Thread all beads.

CONSTRUCTION:
Work this cord 5 in the round to 18". (See pages 6-7.) Finish ends, thread through bead or end caps to attach clasps.

Attach this cord to the Pink bracelet.

Memory Wire Bracelet

Black and white goes with anything and the little touch of pink is so "in style". This fun bracelet keeps its shape and stays on your wrist because it has a memory wire core.

SIZE: 10" including end beads

MATERIALS:
1 spool *Mastex* 774 Rose #18 cord
1 tube each *Miyuki* 8° seed beads (420 White, 420 Black)
2 *Marvin Overman* lampwork beads
2 Pink 6° seed beads
10" *Jane's Fiber and Beads* Memory bracelet wire
Crochet steel hook (*Susan Bates* #4 or *Wright/Boye* #7)
#7 needle
Round-nose Pliers

STRING THE BEADS:
Thread the beads, alternating 1 White bead and 1 Black bead until you have 50" of beads strung.

CONSTRUCTION:
Using pliers, make a small loop at each end of the memory wire. Work the cord around the wire by joining the first round around the wire. It's easier to work around the wire than to put the wire in afterwards. Work the cord until you have just enough space for the lampwork beads at each end. Slip the lampwork bead over the end of the wire.

Thread the tail from the bracelet through the lampwork bead, through the Pink seed bead, and back through the lampwork bead. Push the needle into the cord and knot. Go back through the beads again. Take the thread back through the beads into the cord and knot again.

Work the thread back and forth once or twice, then cut off close to the cord. Repeat this on the other end.

Working a Counted Bead Pattern

It is very important to watch carefully how you thread the beads onto the thread. If one bead is out of place, your pattern will not form properly.

Check your threading pattern every few inches. That way, if you find a mistake, you can correct it quickly.

Blue Bangle

Iridescent sapphire beads bring a bit of sparkle to this simple bracelet. When you need a smaller bangle with subtle elegance, make the pretty pink one.

These are great projects to do when you have strung too many beads and need to use up the leftovers!

SIZE: 7" inside circumference

MATERIALS:
1 spool *Conso* Navy #18 nylon cord
2 tubes *Miyuki* 356c Star Sapphire 8°
   seed beads
Crochet steel hook (*Susan Bates* #4 or
   Wright/Boye #7)
#7 needle

STRING THE BEADS:
Thread beads.

CONSTRUCTION:
   Work this bangle using the same directions as Jane's Sorbet Bangle on page 29.
   Work 5 in the round until 8".
Join the ends together to create a beautiful bangle.

Pretty in Pink Bangle

SIZE: 7" inside circumference

MATERIALS:
1 spool *Coats and Clark* Pink thread
1 tube *Miyuki* 142 Rose Gray 11° seed
   beads
Crochet steel (*Susan Bates* #10 or
   Wright/Boye #11)
#10-12 beading needle

STRING THE BEADS:
Thread beads.

CONSTRUCTION:
   Work this bangle using the same directions as Jane's Sorbet Bangle on page 29.
   Work 5 in the round until 8" long.
   Join the ends together to create a bangle.

Aboriginal Basic Lariat

Highlight those extraordinary lampwork beads by crocheting a rope in a single color that enhances the character of the unique focal beads.

SIZE: 40" including lampwork beads

MATERIALS:
1 spool *Mastex* #780 Chinese Rust #18 Nylon cord
92 grams *Miyuki* F460A Metallic Burgundy 8° seed beads
6 Metallic Burgundy 6° seed beads
4 *JoAnne Zekowski* lampwork beads
Crochet steel hook (*Susan Bates* #4 or *Wright/ Boye* #7)
#7 sharp needle

STRING THE BEADS:
Thread all the 8° beads.

CONSTRUCTION:
Work 5 in the round, leaving an 8"-10" tail, until the cord is 36" long. Work the last round without beads and pull the last loop out about 10". Cut in the middle of loop and pull the working thread back out. This leaves a neat knot.

Attach the lampwork beads by using the tails at each end.

Thread needle onto tail end and run the needle and thread through left hand side of each loop with a bead on it. Pull this up tight. It will pull all the beads to the center, arranging it neatly. The same can be done on the other end by going through the thread at the top of the bead, also arranging it neatly.

Use the same thread to attach the lampwork beads by putting one 6° seed bead between each of the larger beads and one at each end of the largest bead.

At the end, add one 8° and push the needle back through the 6° and the rest of the lampwork to the cord. Push the needle into the cord and knot.

Work thread back and forth once or twice, then cut off close to the cord.

Necklace with Wire

If you prefer a little more stability in your necklaces, crochet around a core of memory wire. The wire helps maintain the desired shape even under the weight of this large lampwork bead.

SIZE: 20" necklace

MATERIALS:

1 spool *Conso* Beige #18 nylon cord
1 spool *Coats & Clark* Light Green #69
2 *Marvin Overman* lampwork beads
1 tube each *Miyuki* (F460k Deep Blue Wine Berry 8°, F631i Olive 11°)
1 strand 3 mm Lime Green Czech fire polish
1 *Jane's Fiber and Beads* Marcasite toggle clasp
18" necklace size Memory wire
Crochet steel hooks (*Susan Bates* #4 & #10 or *Wright/ Boye* #7 & #11)
Needles (#7 sharp, #10 beading)
1 small needle-nose pliers

Necklace:

First cut the wire from spool to 18". Create loops at each ends using the pliers. Grasp the end of the wire with pliers and roll it back on itself.

Make sure that the wire crosses over itself just a bit, then slip one end of the clasp onto the wire. Repeat on the other side.

STRING THE BEADS:

Mix the Blue 8° seed beads and 3 mm fire polish beads together in a small dish. Thread these beads onto the #18 nylon cord. You may have to remove the needle to thread the fire polish beads because their holes are a bit smaller.

CONSTRUCTION:

Using the #4 crochet steel, work 4 in the round, leaving an 8"-10" tail. (See pages 6-7.) It is easier to work around the wire than to put the wire in afterwards. Crochet around the length of the wire.

You want to stretch the beaded cord just a bit to keep the necklace in a less tight shape.

Finish:

Thread the needle with tail and wrap the thread around the loop you created. Thread through the "O" ring of the clasp once or twice then go back and pick up the top thread of each bead in the cord.

Thread back through the beaded cord. Knot and cut.

Repeat for the other end.

Green Spiral:

You are going to make 2 pieces of 4 in the round cord, one 7½" and the other 1" long.

STRING THE BEADS:

Thread the 11°seed beads onto 30" of the #69 Coats and Clark thread.

CONSTRUCTION:

Attach the 7½" cord to the main body of the necklace 4" from the clasp. Attach the smaller bead to the larger bead with the 1" section. Wrap the smaller cord loosely around the body of the main necklace, until the larger bead hangs in the center of the necklace.

Using the Coats & Clark threaded on the beading needle, gently Tack stitch the 7½" cord to the center of the necklace.

Feel free to gently Tack stitch it in a couple of spots.

Crochet with Beads 21

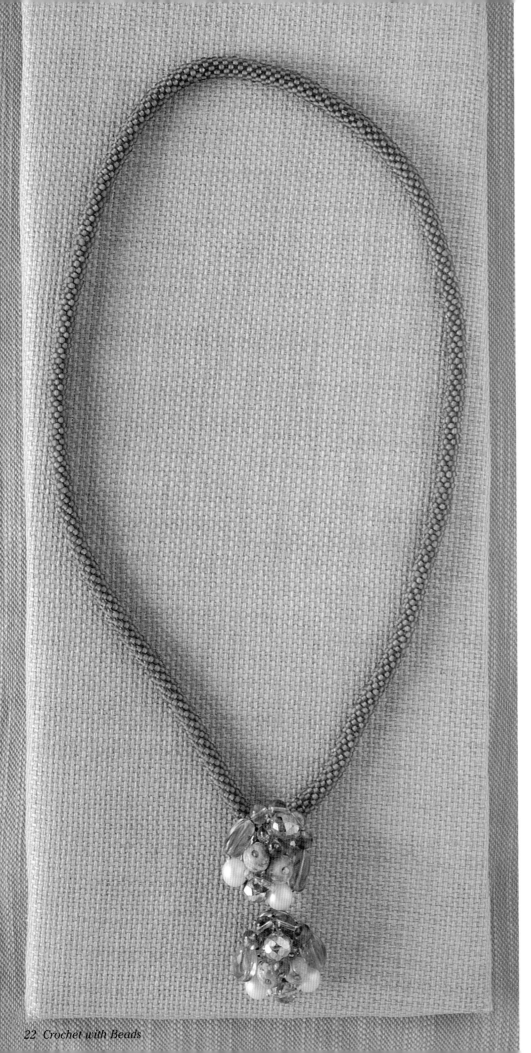

Your Mom's Blue Earring Necklace

This is a fun necklace using those earrings that we all have in the back of our jewelry boxes. We can't bear to part with them because they once belonged to our Mothers or Grandmothers, but we never wear them because they pinch our ears.

This is a way to wear them in remembrance of the women we love. This does not damage the earrings in any way. Showcase those treasures from Grandmother's jewelry box by adding a simple crocheted rope to make an eclectic necklace.

SIZE: 26"

MATERIALS:
1 spool *Coats and Clark* Pale Blue #69 nylon thread
1 hank Matte Gray Czech 11° seed beads
1 pair clip style earrings
Crochet steel hook (*Susan Bates* #10 or *Wright/Boye* #11)
#10-12 beading needle

STRING THE BEADS:
Thread all the beads.

CONSTRUCTION:
Work 5 in the round until the cord is 24". (See pages 6-7.) Finish ends, attach earrings.

Check your earrings to make sure they fit tight. You might have to bend them back into shape. Do this very gently as the metal might have already been stressed.

After finishing the ends using the tails, make a loop of beads around the base of the earring flap, up close to the back of the earring. Make it snug but not too tight, it has to have a little give so it allows a little movement.

Make the loop strong, 2 passes with the needle and thread should do it. Push needle back into the cord. Knot.

Push thread back and forth in the cord again and cut.

Your Mom's Black Earring Necklace

When your evening event requires something special, reach for this iridescent blue rope.

The rich colors are very classy and the earrings add that designer look that will have everyone asking where you bought that gorgeous necklace.

SIZE: 34"

MATERIALS:
1 spool *Coats and Clark* Black #69 nylon thread
1 hank Blue Iris Czech 11° seed beads
1 pair clip style earrings
Crochet steel hook
    (*Susan Bates* #10 or *Wright/Boye* #11)
#10-#12 beading needle

STRING THE BEADS:
Thread all the beads.

CONSTRUCTION:
Work 5 in the round until the cord is 32". (See pages 6-7.) Finish ends, attach earrings.

Check your earrings to make sure they fit tight. You might have to bend them back into shape. Do this very gently as the metal might have already been stressed.

After finishing the ends using the tails, make a loop of beads around the base of the earring flap, up close to the back of the earring.

Make it snug but not too tight. It has to have a little give so it allows a little movement. Make the loop strong. Two passes with the needle and thread should do it. Push needle back into the cord. Knot.

Push thread back and forth in the cord again and cut.

Creating a Loop for a Lariat

Richly elegant matte finish grape seed beads crocheted together create a classy foundation for showing off a multitude of pendants.

SIZE: 22"

MATERIALS:

1 spool *Mastex* 766 Cardinal #18 nylon thread
42-46 grams *Miyuki* F399e Sparkling Grape 8° seed beads
Marvin Overman lampwork beads
1 Silver 7 mm soldered "O" ring
1 *Barley Beads* Quick Switch Bead Post
Crochet steel hook (#4 *Susan Bates* or #7 *Wright/Boye*)

STRING THE BEADS:
Thread the beads.

CONSTRUCTION:

To create a loop of worked cord:

Crochet 3" of 5 in the round cord. (See pages 6-7.) Fold the cord in half. The other end will have a slightly staggered look to it. Keeping the steel in the last worked loop, turn the end with the steel in it to meet the side where the low and higher beads are.

Push the hook onto the low bead loop, cross the thread over and work the two loops off with just the thread. Do the same with the high bead. You have now joined the cord and decreased by 4 stitches. Work the next 3 beads to the left. This will bring you back to the three already worked beads on the other side.

Push the hook through the top thread of the first worked bead, working off loops with another loop with a bead in the middle. Repeat this with the next 2 beads. Decrease this by one more stitch, to bring it back to 5 in the round.

Work two single stitches, then push the hook into the next two loops with beads on them, working one loop with bead in the middle in place of two.

Work 2 more single stitches with beads, then push the hook into 2 loops with beads on them and work these off the same as the last decrease.

This will bring you back to 5 in the round.

Keep the first tail in the middle of your work. Snip it off after about an inch.

Necklace:

Work the rest of the cord at 5 in the round to 21". Stitch the soldered Silver "O" into the end of the finished cord, using the ring to attach the bail from the Quick Switch.

Confetti Bangle Bracelet

Highlight that very special silver charm with a bright mix of colors and beads in several sizes. This bracelet and necklace combination will brighten even the cloudiest winter day.

SIZE: 8"

MATERIALS:

1 spool *Mastex* 722 Natural #18 cord
1 tube each 8° seed beads *Miyuki* (410b
    Purple, 408 Red, 405d Red Orange,
    405a Yellow Orange, 404 Yellow,
    411k Green, 412g Blue Green,
    412D Light Blue, 414 Blue, 402 White)
1 *Kipuka Trading* Silver flower
Crochet steel hook (*Susan Bates* #4 or
    Wright/Boye #7)
#7 needle

STRING:

Mix all the beads together in a bowl. Thread beads onto cord.

CONSTRUCTION:

    Crochet 5 in the round until 8". (See pages 6-7.)
    Join seamlessly. (See page 29.)
    Create a small loop of beads around the finished bangle to attach flower.

Confetti Single-Strand Necklace

Use every color in the rainbow or pick out your favorites to create a cheerful confetti necklace.

SIZE: 26" including clasp

MATERIALS:

1 spool *Mastex* 722 Natural #18 cord
1 tube each *Miyuki* 8° seed beads (410b Purple,
    408 Red, 405d Red Orange, 405a Yellow
    Orange, 404 Yellow, 411k Green, 412g Blue
    Green, 412D Light Blue, 414 Blue, 402 White)
1 *Springall Adventures* Silver clasp
Crochet steel (*Susan Bates* #4 or *Wright/Boye* #7)
#7 needle

STRING THE BEADS:

Mix all the beads together in a bowl. Thread beads onto cord.

CONSTRUCTION:

    Crochet 6 in the round until 25" long.
    Finish the ends. (See pages 6-7.)

Confetti Multi-Strand Necklace

The Confetti Multi-Strand necklace is a truly random mix of all colors of beads.

A separate loop holds a lovely silver charm.

The loop also slides off, making the bead pendant interchangeable.

SIZE:
22" including clasp

MATERIALS:
1 spool *Coats and Clark* Cream #69 thread
1 tube each *Miyuki* 11° seed beads
   (410b Purple, 408 Red,
   405d Red Orange,
   405a Yellow Orange,
   404 Yellow, 411k Green,
   412g Blue Green,
   412D Light Blue,
   414 Blue, 402 White)
1 *Springall Adventures* Silver multi strand clasp
1 *Kipuka Trading* Silver flower
Crochet steel hook
   (*Susan Bates* #10 or
   Wright/Boye #11)
#10 or #12 beading needle

STRING THE BEADS:
Mix all the beads together in a bowl. Thread beads.

CONSTRUCTION:
   Make 4 worked cords, 6 in the round: 21", 20", 19", 3". (See pages 6-7.)
   Finish ends, adding small loops of beads to attach the clasp.
   Join the small loop seamlessly. (See page 29.)
Attach flower to the 3" loop with a ring of beads so it can be threaded on and off the necklace.

Looped Lime Green Necklace

Natural tones of stone, grass, and water soothe the senses when you view or touch this lovely lariat-style necklace. The loop secures the pendant.

SIZE: 21"

MATERIALS:
1 spool *Coats and Clark* Light Green #69 thread
21-23 grams *Miyuki* 399w Mustard Gold 11° seed beads
1 tube *Miyuki* 1165 Gold Green10° triangles
One Gold 6° bead
Marvin Overman lampwork (2 small donuts, 1 larger focal bead)
Crochet steel hook (*Susan Bates* #10 or *Wright/Boye* #11)

STRING THE BEADS:
Mix the 11° seed beads and 10° triangles in a dish. Sting all beads onto thread.

CONSTRUCTION:
To create a loop of worked cord:
Crochet 3" of 5 in the round cord. (See pages 6-7.) Fold the cord in half. The other end will have a slightly staggered look to it. Keeping the hook in the last worked loop, turn the end with the hook in it to meet the side where the low and higher beads are. Push the hook onto the low bead loop, cross the thread over and work the two loops off with just the thread. Do the same with the high bead. You have now joined the cord and decreased by 4 stitches.

Work the next 3 beads to the left. This will bring you back to the three already worked beads on the other side. Push the hook through the top thread of the first worked bead, working off loops with another loop with a bead in the middle. Repeat this with the next 2 beads. Decrease this by one more stitch, to bring it back to 5 in the round.

Work 2 single stitches, then push the hook into the next 2 loops with beads on them, working one loop with bead in the middle in place of two. Work 2 more single stitches with beads, then push the hook into 2 loops with beads on them and work these off the same as the last decrease.

This will bring you back to 5 in the round. Keep the first tail in the middle of your work. Snip it off after about an inch.

Necklace:
Work the rest of the cord at 5 in the round to 16", leaving a 10" tail. Work 2 more sections, 1¼" long.

Attach the two donut beads to the focal bead with the 1" sections and attach to the necklace cord.

Joining a Bangle Seamlessly:

Taking the tails from the beginning thread and the working thread, pull both through the last loop on the steel.

Pull out the working thread loop 10". Cut the working thread loop in the middle and pull the working thread back out. Pull them both tight. This leaves 2 tails 8"-10" in the same loop. Knot these ends together, this forms the bangle.

With the longer thread, thread the needle. Twist the two ends just a bit they will have a slightly staggered look to them. Weave the ends together by using the threaded needle to go into the top of the loop on the most prominent bead.

This should be the first bead from the beginning round. Next, take the needle through the loop of the least prominent bead. This should be the first bead in the very last round.

Continue this process 4 more times.

Take it out if it doesn't look even.

You might have to do it once or twice to get it right, but it's worth it. When you finish the join, pull the needle and thread through the body of the cord. Knot on a loop. Work the thread back and forth through the cord.

Repeat with the other thread.

Jane's Sorbet Bangle

This sorbet bangle bracelet feels wonderful on your wrist. It is comfortable to wear because it is flexible, and easy to make because you don't need a clasp.

The smooth beads feel silky and the subtle colors are glamorous in the evening and pretty for daywear.

SIZE: 7" inside circumference

MATERIALS:
1 spool *Mastex* Flax #18 nylon cord
1 tube each *Miyuki* 6° seed beads (758 Light Gold, 760 Powder Pink Gold, 761 Coral Gold, 762 Apricot Wash Gold, 763 Dusty Pink Gold)
Crochet steel hook (*Susan Bates* #4 or *Wright/Boye* #7)
#7 needle

STRING THE BEADS:
Thread on 72 beads of each color onto cord.

CONSTRUCTION:
Work 5 in the round until finished. (See pages 6-7.) Join ends together to make bangle. To make this bangle shorter or longer, make sure to add or subtract from all the colors, not just one.

For example to add ¼", add 2 each of each of the colors, which equals 10 beads. Make bangle shorter by the same method. Subtract 2 beads from each color.

'Stars and Stripes' Flag Necklace

Thread a necklace or set of bracelets with a patriotic spin using a red-white-and-blue collection of beads, or make an elegant bangle for a black tie affair using gold or silver mixed with black.

SIZE: 22" including clasp

MATERIALS:
1 spool *Conso* Light Brown or
    Caramel #18 cord or
    1 spool *Coats and Clark*
    Cream #69
2 tubes each *Miyuki* 8° seed
    beads (408 Red, 402 White,
    417 Blue)
1 *Jane's Fiber and Beads* Antique
    Gold ball and socket clasp
Crochet steel hook
    (*Susan Bates* #4 or #10 or
    Wright/Boye #7 or #11)
#7 needle or
    #10-#12 beading needle

STRING THE BEADS:
Thread on 3 White, 3 Red, repeat until you have 76 sets of White and 75 sets of Red.
At the end of the Red and White beads, thread on 12 Blue beads. The threading pattern for Blue and White stars follows. B is for Blue, W is for White.
    *WBB   WBW   WBW
WBW BBW BBB
    WBB WBW WBW WBW
BBW BBB
    WBB WBW WBW WBW
BBW BBB
    WBB WBW WBW WBW
BBW BBB
    WBB WBW WBW WBW
BBW BBB *
This pattern creates 10 stars. Repeat * to * 5 times to create 50 stars. Next, add 9 Blue beads.

CONSTRUCTION:
    Work 5 in the round. (See pages 6-7.)
    Use the tails to attach the clasp to the necklace.

Size 11 Beads - Smaller Bangle Bracelet

Make different size bracelets by simply changing the bead size.

SIZE: 8¹/4" inside circumference

MATERIALS:
1 spool *Conso* Light Brown or Caramel #18 cord
1 tube each 11° seed beads *Miyuki*
    (408 Red, 402 White, 417 Blue)
Crochet steel hook (*Susan Bates* #10 or
    Wright/Boye #11)
#7 needle beading needle

STRING THE BEADS:
Thread on 3 White, 3 Red, until you have 25" of strung beads.
At the end of the Red and White beads, thread on 12 Blue beads.
The threading pattern for Blue and White stars follows. B is for Blue, W is for White.
    *WBB WBW WBW WBW BBW BBB
    WBB WBW WBW WBW BBW BBB
    WBB WBW WBW WBW BBW BBB
    WBB WBW WBW WBW BBW BBB
    WBB WBW WBW WBW BBW BBB*

CONSTRUCTION:
    Repeat * to * 3 times. Next, add 9 Blue beads.
    Work 5 in the round. (See pages 6-7)
    Join the bangle seamlessly. (See page 29.)

Size 8 Beads - Larger Bangle

SIZE: 8¹/2" inside circumference

MATERIALS:
1 spool *Coats and Clark* Cream #69
1 tube each *Miyuki* 8° seed beads
    (408 Red, 402 White, 417 Blue)
Crochet steel hook (*Susan Bates* #4 or
    Wright/Boye #7)
#10-#12 beading needle

STRING THE BEADS:
Thread on 3 White, 3 Red, until you have 38 sets of White, 37 sets of Red.
At the end of the Red and White beads, thread on 12 Blue beads.
The threading pattern for Blue and White stars follows. B is for Blue, W is for White.
    *WBB WBW WBW WBW BBW BBB
    WBB WBW WBW WBW BBW BBB
    WBB WBW WBW WBW BBW BBB
    WBB WBW WBW WBW BBW BBB
    WBB WBW WBW WBW BBW BBB*

CONSTRUCTION:
    Repeat * to * once.
    Next, add 9 Blue beads.
    Work 5 in the round. (See pages 6-7.)
    Join the bangle seamlessly. (See page 29.)

Striped Bangle

Add stripes for color variation.

SIZE: 8" inside circumference

MATERIALS:
1 spool *Conso* Red #18 cord
1 strand each *Bead World* Indonesian lampwork
    donuts (1 Red Stripe, 1 Yellow Stripe)

Crochet steel hook (*Susan Bates* #4 or *Wright/Boye* #7)
#7 needle

STRING:
Thread onto cord:
2 Red, 2 Yellow, * repeat * until all beads are threaded.

CONSTRUCTION:
    Work 4 in the round until worked cord is 8" long. (See pages 6-7)
    Join seamlessly. (See page 29.)
    Knot the ends into the cord.
    Weave the thread back and forth once or twice and cut off.

Many thanks to Martha Pafralides for helping design this pattern.

Chunky Necklace

Add a bit of drama to your wardrobe with this charming, chunky necklace. Smooth donut beads make an eye-catching piece.

SIZE: 22"

MATERIALS:
1 spool *Mastex* 770 Leaf #18 cord
Bead World Indonesian lamp work beads (5 strands 7-9 mm donuts, 3 large lampwork beads)
1 Black 8° seed bead
Crochet steel hook (*Susan Bates* #4 or *Wright/Boye* #7)
#7 needle

STRING THE BEADS:
Thread all the beads onto the cord.

CONSTRUCTION:
Work 4 in the round for 16". (See pages 6-7.)

Finish the ends.

At one end create a loop of lampwork beads just large enough to go around the lampwork bead at the other end.

To make the loop strong, go through twice with the needle and thread.

Knot into worked cord and snip the end off.

Attach larger beads to the other end using the tail.

Big Bead Bangle Bracelet

You can wear fun beaded bracelets for any occasion. This particular pattern allows you to show off all the pattern on a rondel bead, not just the edges.

SIZE: 8"

MATERIALS:
1 spool *Conso* Navy #18 cord
Bead World Indonesian lampwork beads (3 strands 5-7 mm Blue striped donuts, 1 large bead)
Crochet steel hook (*Susan Bates* #4 or *Wright/Boye* #7)
#7 needle

STRING THE BEADS: Thread the beads onto the cord.

CONSTRUCTION:
Work 5 in the round to 7½". (See pages 6-7.) Finish both ends using tails to secure the larger bead in the middle by passing the thread from both ends back and forth a couple of times.

Knot the ends into the cord. Weave the thread back and forth once or twice and cut off.

Mixed Size Bead Bangle Bracelet

Make a beautiful bangle bracelet with a random mix of gorgeous glass beads.

SIZE: 8"

MATERIALS:
1 spool *Mastex* 772 Slate #18 nylon cord
115 mixed size Czech beads
Crochet steel (*Susan Bates* #4 or
      Wright/Boye #7)
#7 needle

STRING THE BEADS:
Thread beads onto the cord.

CONSTRUCTION:
      Work 4 in the round until you have 8". (See pages 6-7.)
      Finish the ends and join seamlessly to create a bangle. (See page 29.)

Mixed Size Bead Necklace

Three hundred fifty mixed glass beads never looked so good! This artsy collection of Czech beads can be strung at random or meticulously planned for stunning effects.

The mix of color makes this the perfect accessory to match any outfit.

SIZE: 22"

MATERIALS:
1 spool *Mastex* 757 Flax #18 nylon cord
350 mixed size Czech beads
1 *Springall Adventures* large Silver clasp
Crochet steel (*Susan Bates* #4 or
      Wright/Boye #7)
#7 needle

STRING THE BEADS:
Thread beads onto the cord.

CONSTRUCTION:
      Work 4 in the round until 21" in length. (See pages 6-7)
      Watch your stitches with this one. It's really easy to drop the stitches. Finish. (See pages 6-7.)
      Attach clasp with the tails.

Mixing Beads

The easiest method is to simply pour all the beads into a bowl and thread them onto the cord. This method is particularly useful if you are using your leftover beads.

If you have purchased beads in separate containers, you can distribute your beads more randomly over the necklace or bracelet if you pour each container evenly into 4 different bowls. Mix up the beads and string them one bowl at a time.

FOCUS ON PIANO
A Concise Approach to Learning and Playing

LESSONS • THEORY • TECHNIQUE • SOLOS

Written, Arranged,
and Engraved by
JONATHON ROBBINS

Production, Design &
Marketing Consultant
GAIL HOPKINS KOLEHMA

Executive Editor &
Managing Director
TONY SANTORELLA

Instructional Performance CD
Recorded by L.A. Studio Pro
DEAN MORA

Recorded at Angel City Studios
Los Angeles, California
by Chief Engineer
CHRIS TEDESCO

Graphic Design, Cover &
Electronic Production
CAROLYN M. CONNORS

focus

SANTORELLA
PUBLICATIONS, LTD.

Table of Contents

Table of Contents

Table of Contents

Level 1

Introducing the Piano

Introducing Notation

The Right Hand

First Melodies

The Left Hand

Chords

The G Seventh Chord

Playing the C and G7 Chords

Melody and Accompaniment

The F Chord

The Pick-up Measure & Rests

Five Finger Patterns for Two Hands

Augmentation Dots & 3/4 Time

The Repeat Sign

Tempo

The Eighth Note

Sharps, Half Steps & Whole Steps

Scales and Key Signatures

Playing the F♯

Principal Chords of G Major

1st and 2nd Ending Repeats

New Hand Position in C Major

Evening Stroll

Kum Ba Ya

Down by the Riverside

The Dotted Quarter Note

Cockles and Mussels (Molly Malone)

Broken Chords

Introducing the Piano

The Keyboard

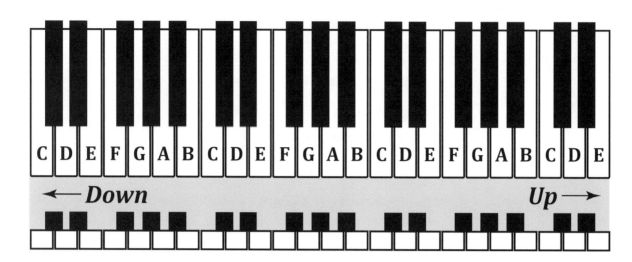

The Names of the Notes
A ♦ B ♦ C ♦ D ♦ E ♦ F ♦ G

There are only seven letter names for the musical notes. They are the first seven letters of the alphabet - the letters A, B, C, D, E, F & G. The graphic above represents a portion of the keyboard.

The complete piano keyboard is made up of 88 Keys. The lowest note (to the left) is the note, "A." Locate it now, and start playing up the keyboard. Name the notes while you play; they are arranged exactly like the alphabet. When you reach the note, "G," start over with "A."

As you play, listen to each sound. The keys on the left of the keyboard are the lower notes. As you play up the keyboard, that is, to the right, you'll notice that the notes get higher.

The Black Keys

The piano keyboard has both white keys and black keys.
The black keys are organized in groups of two and groups of three.

Two Black Keys

Find all of the groups of two black keys on the piano and play them from lowest to highest.

Three Black Keys

Now, find all of the groups of three black keys on the piano and play them from lowest to highest.

Middle C & the Notes D & E

The white key to the left of the group of two black keys is the note, "C." Find and play all of the C's on the piano. The "C" that is closest to the center of the keyboard is called, "Middle C." Find and play Middle C.

The white key to the right of the group of two black keys is the note, "E," and the white key between the two black keys is the note, "D." Find and play all of the D's and E's on the piano keyboard.

The Notes F, G, A & B

The white key to the left of the group of three black keys is the note, "F." The white key to the right of the group of three black keys is the note, "B." Find and play all of the F's and B's on the piano keyboard.

The two white keys between the group of three black keys are the notes, "G" & "A." Now find and play all of the G's and A's on the keyboard.

Introducing the Piano

Keyboard Chart

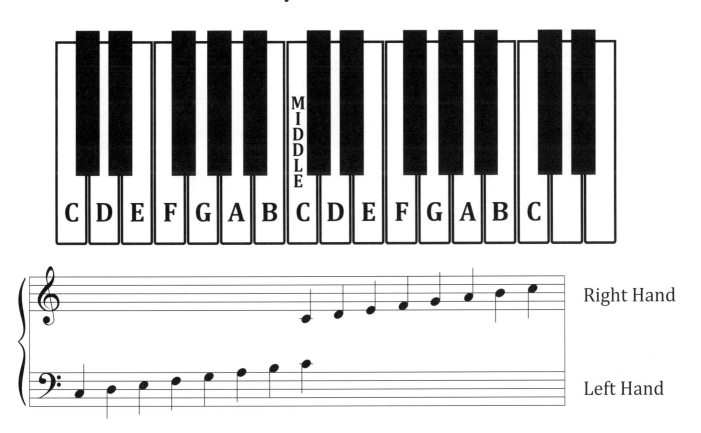

Right Hand

Left Hand

The chart above shows the relationship between the keyboard and the written notes. You'll learn more about music notation on the pages that follow. The notes on the Treble Staff (the top line of music) are often played with the right hand, while the notes on the Bass Staff (the bottom line), are often played with the left hand. Notice how Middle C is written on each staff above. These two written notes represent the same key on the piano. In beginning piano music, Middle C may be played with either hand.

The Hands

In piano music, numbers are often written above or below the notes, to suggest which finger to use.

The fingers of the right and left hands are numbered as shown in the diagram to the right. The thumb is the first finger on both hands.

While many times there is more than one way to play a piece of music, it's often a good idea to follow the suggested fingering when reading and learning a piece for the first time.

The hands should be slightly cupped, with the fingers rounded so that the keys are stuck with the soft pad of the finger tips. The thumb, too, should be rounded so that the keys are struck with the soft pad on the outside of the nail.

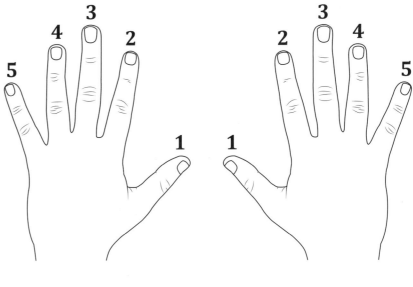

LEFT HAND   RIGHT HAND

Introducing Notation

The Staff

The STAFF is made up of five lines and four spaces. NOTES are written on the lines and spaces of the staff.

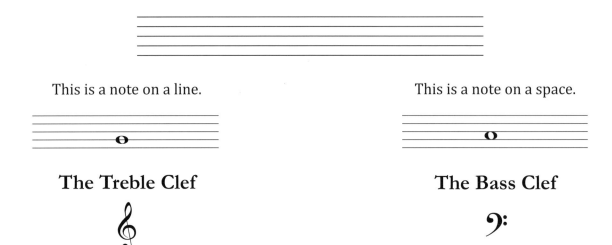

This is a note on a line.

This is a note on a space.

The Treble Clef

The Bass Clef

When a TREBLE CLEF is placed on the Staff, it becomes a TREBLE STAFF. Piano music generally uses the Treble Staff for the higher notes, which are usually played with the right hand.

When a BASS CLEF is placed on the Staff, it becomes a BASS STAFF. Piano music generally uses the Bass Staff for the lower notes, which are usually played with the left hand.

THE TREBLE STAFF

THE BASS STAFF

The Grand Staff

When a Treble Staff and a Bass Staff are joined by a BRACE, the result is a GRAND STAFF. Most piano music is written on the Grand Staff. The higher notes are written toward the top part of the staff, while the lower notes are written toward the bottom part of the staff.

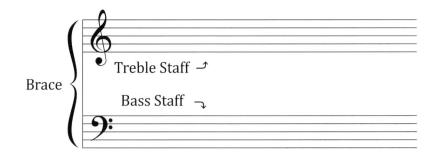

Brace { Treble Staff ↰

Bass Staff ↳

The Measure

The BEAT is the fundamental unit of time in music. On the Staff, Beats are grouped into MEASURES, which are separated by BARLINES (Sometimes spelled, "Bar Lines"). There can be any number of Beats in each Measure (but usually two, three, or four). At the end of a piece of music, you'll find a special type of Barline called a DOUBLE BARLINE.

Barline   Barline   Double Barline
↓   ↓   ↓

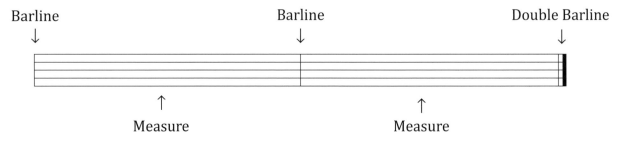

↑   ↑
Measure   Measure

Introducing Notation

The Notes

As we've seen, notes are placed on the lines and spaces of the staff. The placement of the note on the staff indicates the pitch of that note, and which key to play on the piano. The other thing we need to know when playing music is how long to hold each note. This is determined by the type of note we see on the staff. Notes are named in much the same way that fractions are named. We'll start with three basic types of notes:

THE WHOLE NOTE   THE HALF NOTE   THE QUARTER NOTE

The round part of the Note is called the NOTE HEAD and the vertical line (when present) is called the STEM. It's also no coincidence that the notes are named like fractions. Take a look below and you'll see why.

Now the names of the notes make more sense. The Half Note is half as long in duration as the Whole Note, and the Quarter Note is half as long in duration as the Half Note, or only one-quarter as long as the Whole Note.

The Time Signature

OK, now that we know the relationship between the basic notes, we need something else that tells us exactly how long to hold each note. We've already learned that the basic unit of time in music is the Beat. Think of a Beat as time clicking away steadily on a clock, except the clicks can be as slow or as fast as we want them to be, as long as we keep them steady. Once we have that basic Beat established, the only other thing we need to know is now many Beats do we hold each note. The TIME SIGNATURE gives us this information.

The Time Signature consists of two numbers, one on top of the other. It appears at the beginning of each piece of music. The top number of the Time Signature tells us how many beats there are in each Measure, while the bottom number indicates which type of note is to receive the basic unit of one Beat.

Here's an example of the 4/4 Time Signature (pronounced, "four-four time").

4 There are 4 Beats in each Measure
4 The Quarter Note receives one Beat

Now we have a clear picture of exactly how many beats each of the note types above are to receive.

So ... in 4/4 Time we see that ...

The Quarter Note (♩) receives 1 Beat - The Half Note (♩) receives 2 Beats - The Whole Note (o) receives 4 Beats

At first, clap or tap the rhythm of each new piece of music while counting the beats out loud. Then, while playing each new piece, continue to count out loud. This will help you to build a solid rhythm foundation.

The Right Hand

In most beginning piano music, the right hand usually plays the melody. The melody may consist of a single line of notes, perhaps there may also be a harmony line under the melody, and in other cases there may be full chords. We're going to begin with a single melody line, so let's jump right in and get started.

Place your right hand on the keyboard with your thumb (1st finger) on Middle C, as shown in the diagram. Notice the small numbers under the notes. These numbers show which finger to use on each note. You may see them either above or below the note on both the Treble Staff and the Bass Staff, depending on what other notation is on the page. Let's begin with these three exercises:

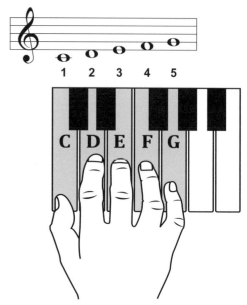

1. Play the five notes up the scale: C, D, E, F, G.
2. Play the five notes down the scale: G, F, E, D, C.
3. Play all five notes up, then down: C, D, E, F, G, F, E, D, C.

NOW, WE'LL PLAY THE SAME EXERCISES WHILE READING THE NOTES ON THE STAFF:

CD Track 2

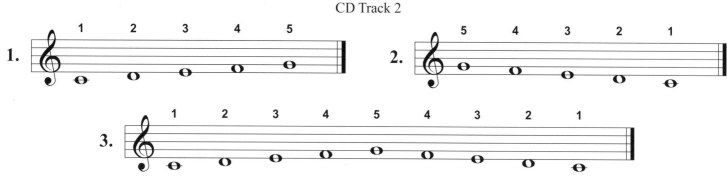

Counting

Try counting and clapping the rhythm of the following three tunes. This is the best way to develop a good sense of rhythm. The counts for each beat is written under the notes. They're all in 4/4 Time, so remember,

The Quarter Note (♩) = 1 beat - The Half Note (♪) = 2 beats - The Whole Note (o) = 4 beats

Frère Jacques

Au Clair de la Lune

Ode to Joy

First Melodies

Now that we've played our first five notes and have worked through the rhythm of some basic melodies, let's play them on the piano from the written music on the Grand Staff. Place your right thumb (1st finger) on Middle C, as before, and let's begin. You may find it helpful to say the notes out loud as you play them. We've written the fingerings above the notes and the count for the beats below.

Frère Jacques

French Folk Song

Au Clair de la Lune

French Folk Song

The Slur

A SLUR is a curved line above or below a group of notes. It indicates that the notes are to be played as a phrase (a musical sentence) in a smooth and connected manner.

Ode to Joy

CD Track 3

L. V. Beethoven

* This type of Double Barline (above) is used to indicate the end of a section, but not the entire composition.

The Left Hand

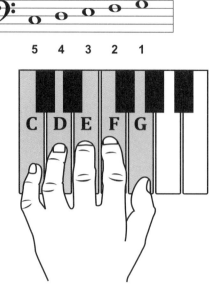

Now, we'll get the left hand playing. Most of the time, the left hand will be playing accompaniment, often in the form of chords and harmony. Before we get to that, we need to practice playing single notes with the left hand.

Place your left hand on the keyboard, with your pinky (5th finger) on the C below Middle C, as shown in the illustration to the left. Just as before, fingering number appear below the notes. This time, we'll be reading notes on the Bass Staff.

When you're ready, start with the exercises below. You can see that they are the same as those you just played with your right hand.

1. Play the five notes up the scale: C, D, E, F, G.
2. Play the five notes down the scale: G, F, E, D, C.
3. Play all five notes up, then down: C, D, E, F, G, F, E, D, C.

PLAY THE SAME EXERCISES WHILE READING THE NOTES ON THE STAFF:

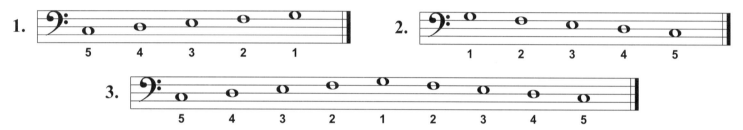

Now play these two melodies with your left hand. Don't forget to count!

Frère Jacques

CD Track 4

French Folk Song

Au Clair de la Lune

French Folk Song

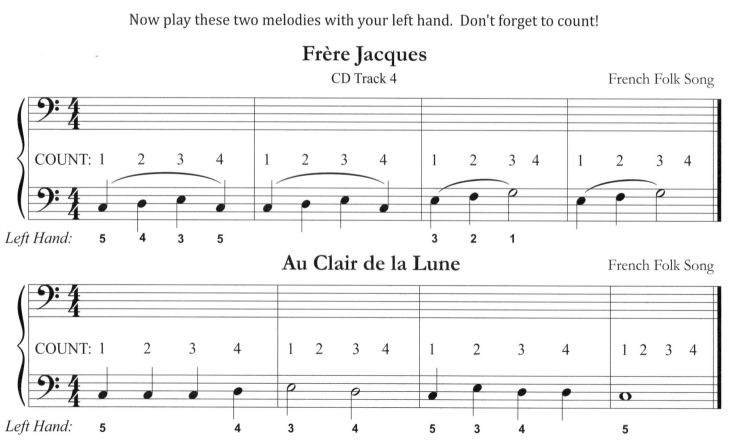

Chords

A CHORD is simply a combination of two or more musical notes. The notes of a Chord may be played at the same time, as a SOLID CHORD, or they may be played consecutively, as a BROKEN CHORD. Chords are often played in many different positions and locations on the keyboard. We'll discuss more about that later when we discuss Chord Theory, but for now, we'll begin with some basic Chord positions and locations. Let's begin by concentrating on playing Chords with the left hand, although Chords can be played with either hand.

The C Chord (C)

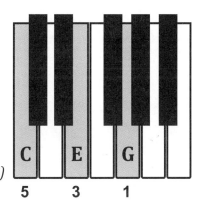

The C Chord (notated with the symbol, "C"), uses the same hand position that we learned on the previous page. It is played with the 5th, 3rd, and 1st fingers of the **LEFT HAND** on the notes, C, E, and G. Take a look at the diagram to the right, then practice the exercises below to get used to playing the Solid C Chord and Broken C Chord in various combinations. Notice the "C" chord symbol above the notes.

(Left Hand)

Chord Studies

CD Track 5

1. Solid Chords

Write in the Count:

2. Broken Chords

Write in the Count:

3. Broken Chords

Write in the Count:

4. Solid & Broken

Write in the Count:

Practice each hand separately in the following exercise before playing them together. Don't forget to count!

CD Track 6

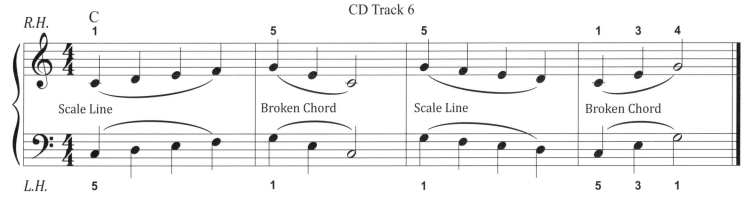

- 13 -

The G Seventh Chord (G7)

New Note - B

The G7 Chord uses a new note "B," which is one note lower than C. This chord also uses an extended hand position, meaning that the note span is greater than five. The note, "G" is a COMMON TONE in both the C and G7 Chords. To play this chord, use your 1st and 2nd finger on the notes G and F, then extend your 5th finger down to the note, B. Find all of the G7 Chords on the keyboard, then play the combination of C - G7 - C in various locations.

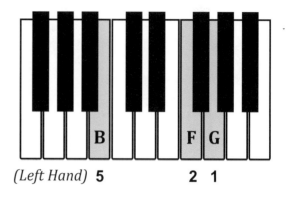

(Left Hand) **5** **2 1**

Chord Studies

CD Track 7

(When writing chord symbols above notes, it is common practice to write the symbol only when the chord changes)

1. **Solid Chords**

2. **Broken Chords**

3. **Solid & Broken**

4. **C & G7 Chords**

Ode to Joy

CD Track 8

Ludwig van Beethoven

R.H.

L.H.

Playing the C and G7 Chords

These melodies feature the C and G7 Chords in the left hand. The right hand part uses the basic five finger position with the first finger on Middle C. Use the same fingering in the left hand as in the previous examples.

Three Blind Mice

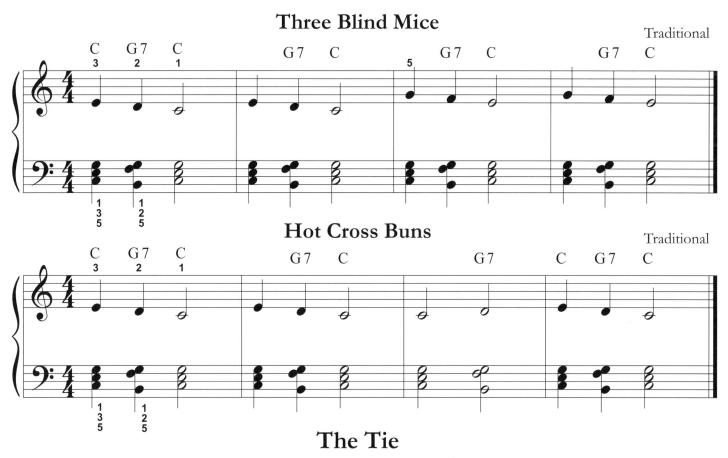

Hot Cross Buns

The Tie

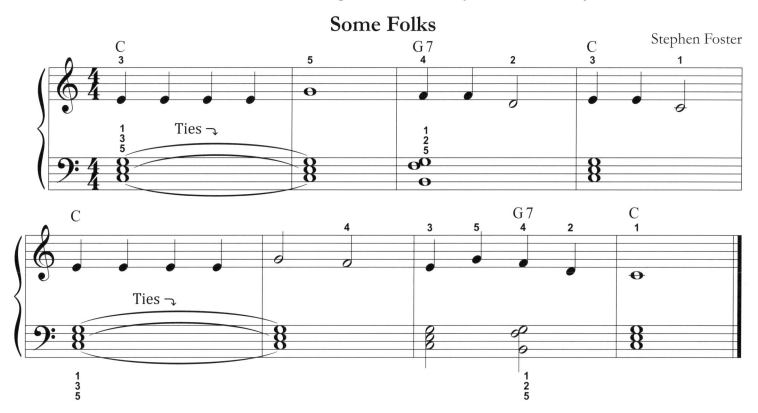

A Tie is a curved line connecting two notes of the same pitch and letter name. As you can see, the same line is used for both Slurs and Ties, however, when the line connects two notes of the same pitch, this tells you to play the first note and hold it for the total number of beats of both notes, without re-striking. A Tie is necessary to hold a note beyond the barline.

1 2 1 2

Some Folks

- 15 -

Melody and Accompaniment

The MELODY of a piece is the tune or lead part. In a song, you would sing the lyrics of the Melody. The Melody contains only one note at a time; the rest of the notes are part of the ACCOMPANIMENT. Just as it sounds, the Accompaniment compliments (or accompanies) the Melody. The Accompaniment may contain a harmony composed of chords, a bass-line, or a counter-melody, or it may contain all three of these components. The Melody is generally the most important and most recognizable part of the piece. It's the part you want to hear most clearly, therefore, play the Accompaniment a little softer than the Melody, so it will stand out.

Lightly Row

CD Track 9

The F Chord (F)

New Note - A

The F Chord also uses an extended hand position and has a new note, "A," for the 1st finger. The 5th finger remains on the note C for both the C and the F Chords, which is a Common Tone in both Chords. Now, find and play all of the F Chords on the keyboard and then play the chord combination of C - F - C - G7 - C.

(Left Hand)

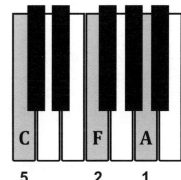

Chord Studies
CD Track 10

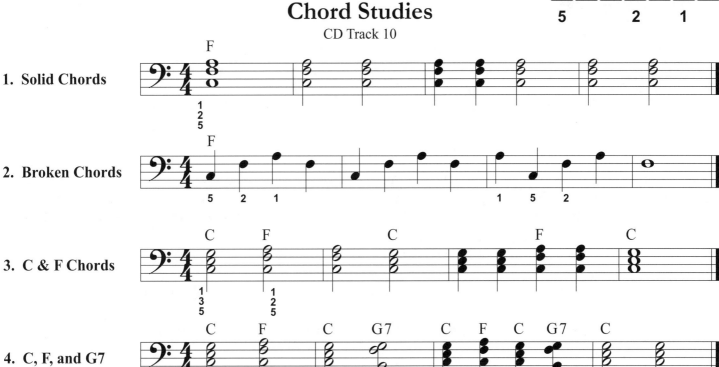

1. **Solid Chords**

2. **Broken Chords**

3. **C & F Chords**

4. **C, F, and G7**

Little Piece
CD Track 11

Antonio Diabelli

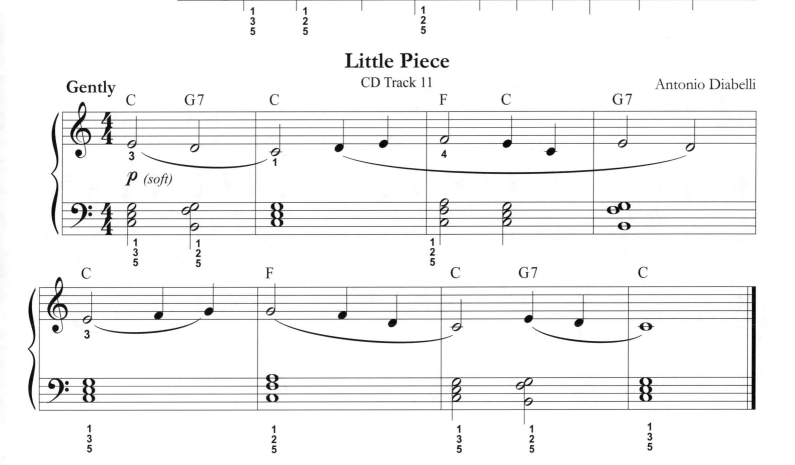

- 17 -

The Pick-up Measure & Rests

The Pick-up

Some compositions do not begin on the first beat of the measure, but instead, begin with a partial measure. This partial measure is called an ANACRUSIS (commonly know as the PICK-UP MEASURE). When a piece contains a Pick-up Measure, there must be a partial measure at the end to complete the Pick-up Measure. This does not alter the Time Signature, even though the Pick-up does not contain the full number of beats.

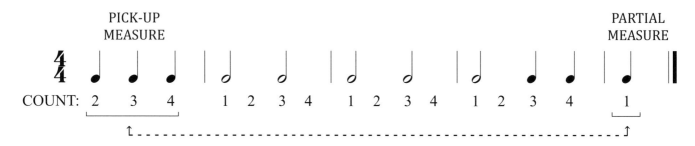

Rests

RESTS are musical symbols used to indicate a number of beats of silence. They are named in the same way as notes, with different symbols being used to indicate the duration of the rests. The names and durations correspond to the note of the same name, so in 4/4 Time, each rest would receive the number of beats below.

Whole Rest (▬) = 4 Beats of silence ... Whole Note (o) = 4 Beats of sound

Half Rest (▬) = 2 Beats of silence ... Half Note (♩) = 2 Beats of sound

Quarter Rest (𝄽) = 1 Beat of silence ... Quarter Note (♩) = 1 Beat of sound

When the Saints Go Marching In

CD Track 12

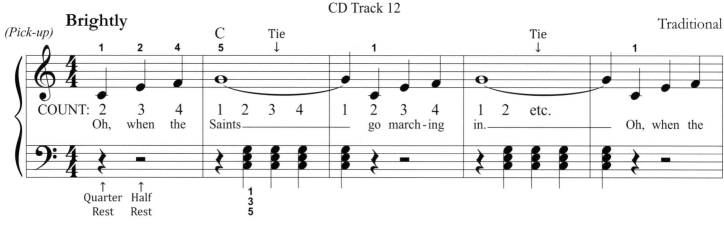

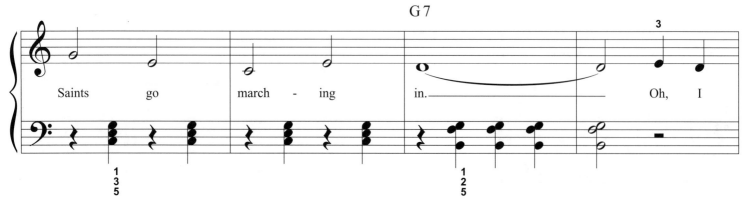

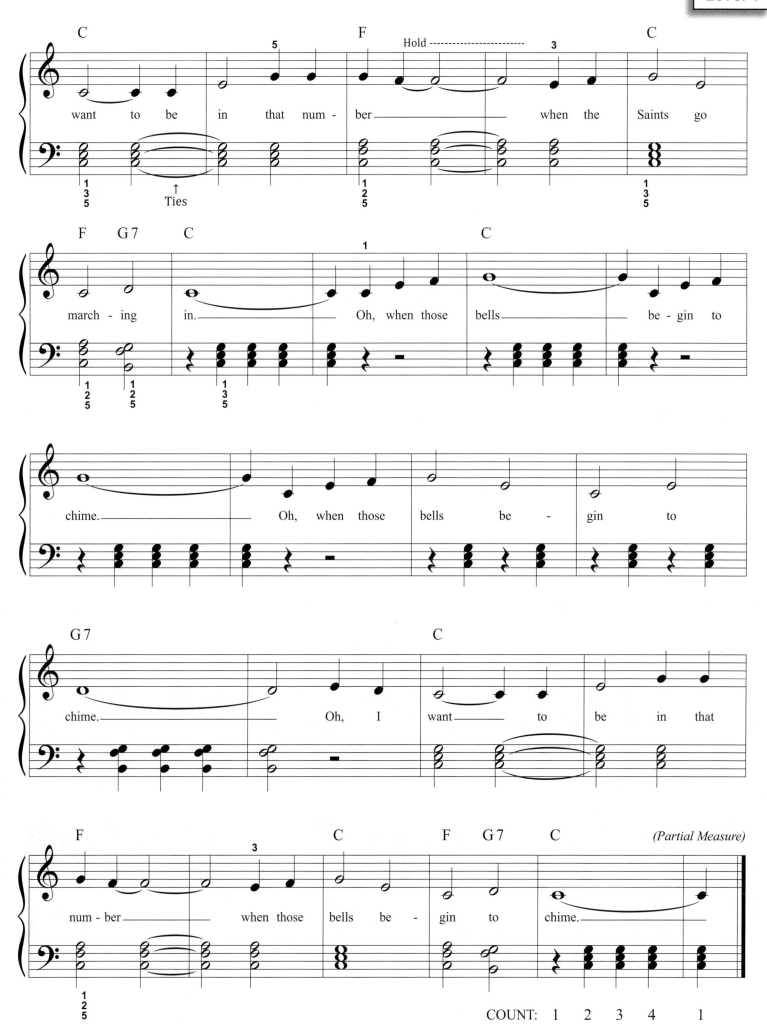

Five Finger Pattern for Two Hands

This new position uses both hands, with the 1st finger (thumb) of both hands on Middle C. Each hand will play the five keys they cover, with the right hand extending up to G and the left hand extending down to F. The pieces that follow contain only a single melody line, with some of the notes being played with the right hand and others with the left. This will allow you to get used to this new hand position. Play the melody smoothly in one phrase as indicated by the added slurs.

There's a duet part added to the piece below. After you learn the melody, have an experienced pianist play along with you. It's not only fun, but it's also a great way to develop a sense of rhythm.

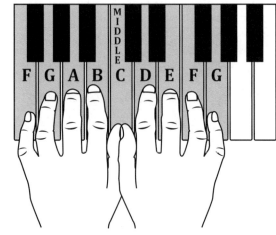

Dynamic Markings

On the previous pages, you've seen some DYNAMIC MARKINGS (the bold letters in the beginning of the piece which tell you how loud or soft to play). They are abbreviations for Italian terms to indicate the volume level.

p = piano (soft)   *mp* = mezzo piano (medium soft)   *mf* = mezzo forte (medium loud)   *f* = forte (loud)

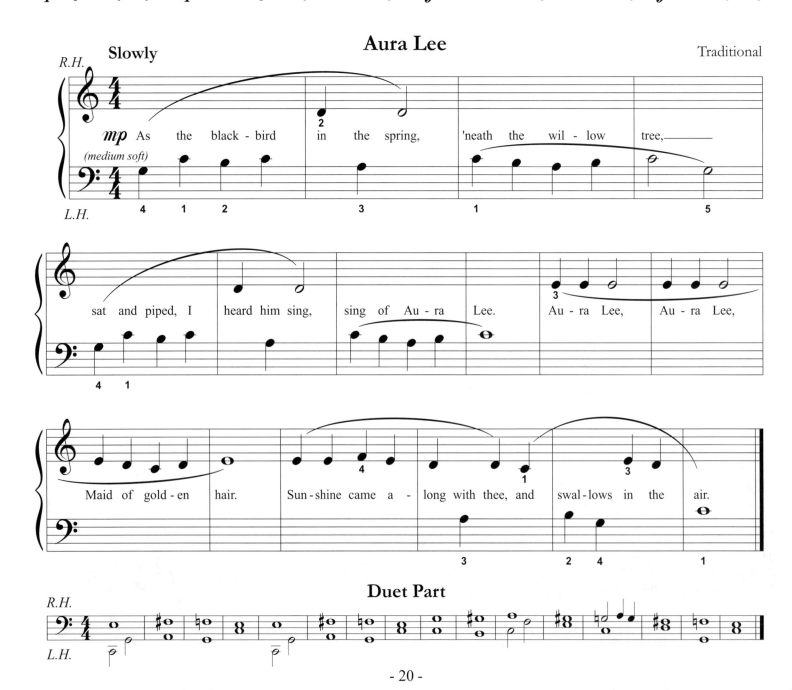

-20-

Augmentation Dots & 3/4 Time

The Augmentation Dot

The AUGMENTATION DOT (or simply, "DOT"), adds one-half of the value of the note. When you played, "When the Saints Go Marching In," you may recall there were quite a few tied notes. Some of these were necessary, since they extended over the barline, but others could have been notated with Dotted Notes instead. The symbol for the Dot is simply just that, a small dot added directly after the Note Head. Take a look at how the Augmentation Dot affects the value of the Half Note below:

If the Half Note (𝅗𝅥) receives 2 Beats   ... then .....   The Dotted Half Note (𝅗𝅥.) receives 3 Beats

The 3/4 Time Signature

The 3/4 Time Signature has a 3 as the top number. As you know, this tells us how many Beats are in each Measure, in this case, 3. Since the bottom number is 4, the Quarter Note still receives 1 Beat. With only 3 Beats in each Measure, you can see that the Dotted Half Note will fit in quite well, and fill the entire Measure.

3 There are 3 Beats in each Measure
4 The Quarter Note receives one Beat

The Strawberry Roan
CD Track 13
Cowboy Song

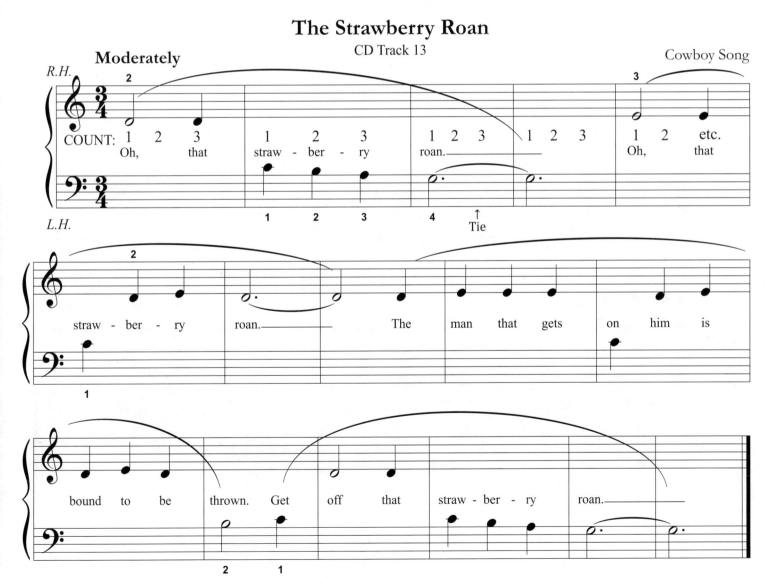

The 3/4 Time Signature is common in waltzes and other traditional dances.

The Repeat Sign

REPEAT SIGNS are placed at the beginning and end of a passage that is to be repeated. They look a lot like Double Barlines with the addition of the two dots facing toward the repeated section. When you arrive at the Back Repeat Sign (the second one), simply return to the Forward Repeat Sign and play that section again. When the Back Repeat Sign is on the last measure, the piece is over after the second playing. It is common not to use a Forward Repeat Sign on the first measure, but we'll put them in now, so you can get used to playing them.

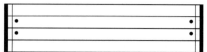

Down in the Valley

American Folk Song

Moderato (*Moderately*)

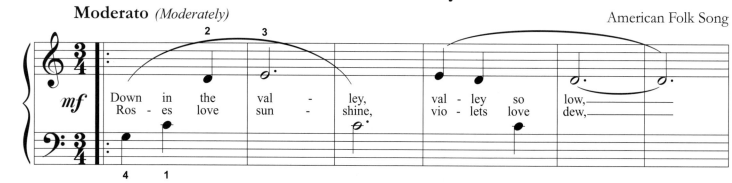

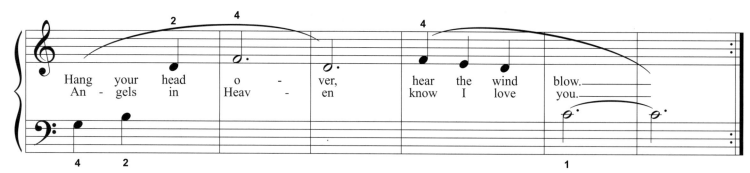

Michael, Row the Boat Ashore

Traditional Spiritual

Moderately Slow

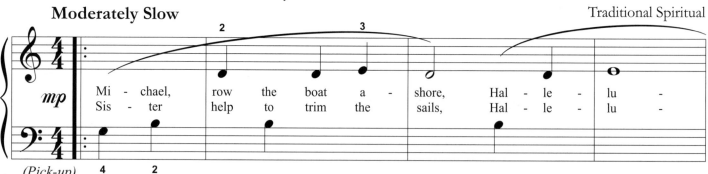

(Pick-up)

(Partial Measure)

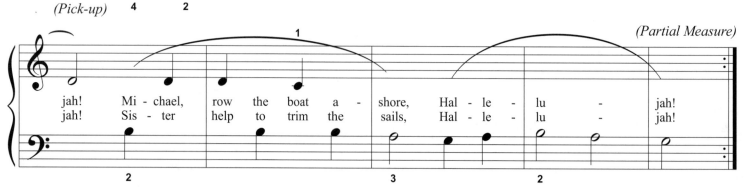

Duet Part

Tempo

By now, you've noticed the text written above the Time Signature at the beginning of each piece. It's there to give you an idea as to the TEMPO of the composition. Tempo means how fast or how slowly to play. The words used to describe the Tempo may be in English or, more commonly, Italian. They're not exact, instead, they suggest a relative range that each piece should be played. Here's a few of the common ones you may see:

← SLOWER   **FASTER →**

Lento	**Adagio**	**Andante**	**Moderato**	**Allegretto**	**Allegro**	**Presto**
(Slowly)	*(Moderately Slow)*	*(Walking Pace)*	*(Moderately)*	*(Moderately Fast)*	*(Fast and Bright)*	*(Very Fast)*

These next examples use a different hand position for your left hand, with your 5th finger on C below Middle C.

Merrily We Roll Along

Traditional

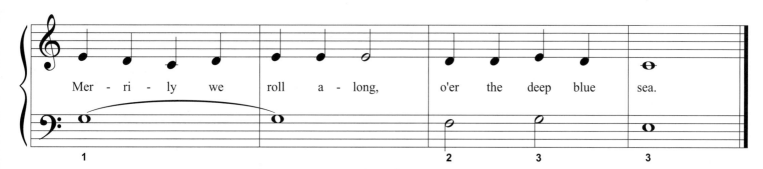

Sleep, Baby Sleep

CD Track 14

German Lullaby

Did you count as you played the pieces above? This is particularly important when playing with both hands.

The Eighth Note

This is an EIGHTH NOTE, as it appears by itself.

Two Eighth Notes together are connected with a BEAM.

Two Eighth Notes equal one Quarter Note.

The EIGHTH REST has the same value as an Eighth Note.

In the beginning, count the Beats which contain Eighth Notes like this ...

1 & 2 & 3 & 4 &

Later, when you are more comfortable with the division of the Beat, count like this ...

1   2   3   4

Eighth Note Exercise
CD Track 15

COUNT: 1 & 2 & 3 & 4 &   1 & 2 & 3 & 4 &   1 & 2 & 3 & 4 &   1 & 2 & 3 & 4 &

Boogie Road

Jonathon Robbins

1 & 2 &   & 4 &   1 & 2 & 3 & 4 &   1   2   3   4

Did you notice that the above piece requires you to change hand positions in both hands?

Sharps, Half Steps & Whole Steps

The Sharp

 This is a SHARP sign. When you see it before a note on the Staff, like this ...

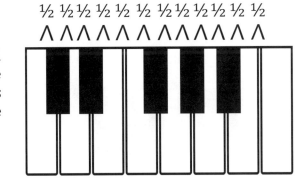

... play that note one Half Step higher. This note is pronounced, "F sharp."

In order to understand how to play this note, let's first talk about HALF STEPS and WHOLE STEPS.

The Half Step

You know that the Piano Keyboard is made up of white keys and black keys. The distance between any two touching keys is one Half Step. It doesn't matter whether one key is black and one is white, or if they are both white. As long as they are touching, the distance between them is one Half Step.

Now, let's take a look at the note, F sharp (F♯) again

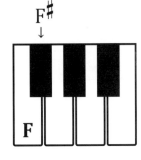

We had learned very early that the higher notes are toward the right end of the keyboard, in other words, as we play notes further to the right, the pitch gets higher. Since the Sharp Sign raises the note by one Half Step, and a Half Step is the distance between any two touching notes, to play F sharp, you would find the note, F, and play the Black Key directly to its right, as shown in the illustration.

The Whole Step

A WHOLE STEP is made up of two consecutive Half Steps.
Any two notes which are one Whole Step apart will have one note in between them.

Take a look at some of the notes on both the kayboard and the staff which are one Whole Step apart.

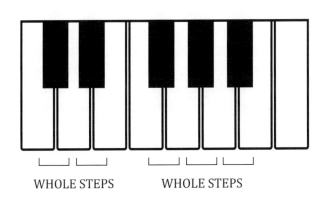

WHOLE STEPS   WHOLE STEPS

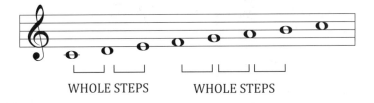

WHOLE STEPS   WHOLE STEPS

Can you see that not all of White Keys are one Whole Step apart? Some have no Black Key in between them.

Remember, as long as there is one key between them, a Whole Step can occur between two white keys, two black keys, or a white key and a black key.

The main thing to remember is that as long as there is one key in between (or skipped), that disance is a Whole Step.

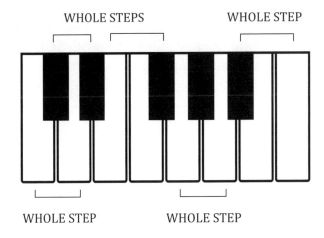

WHOLE STEP   WHOLE STEP

Scales and Key Signatures

The Scale

A SCALE is a series of notes in stepwise succession which are arranged alphateically. There are various types of Scales, but the most common, and the type we'll begin with is the MAJOR SCALE. To be a Major Scale, the notes must be arranged in a specific pattern of Whole Steps and Half Steps, as indicated below.

Whole - Whole - Half - Whole - Whole - Whole - Half

C Major Scale

A Major Scale which begins on the note, C, is called a C MAJOR SCALE. It's played entirely on the white keys. Take a look at the pattern of Whole and Half Steps for this Scale on both the keyboard and the staff.

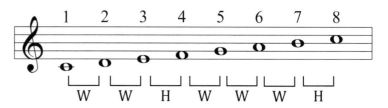

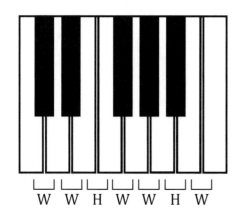

As you can see, there is a Half Step between the 3rd & 4th and the 7th & 8th notes of the Scale. A Major Scale may begin on any note, as long as the pattern remains the same. Next, we'll look at a Major Scale which begins on a different note.

G Major Scale

Here's a Major Scale beginning on G. This scale is not played entirely on the white keys. It uses the black key, F-sharp, which we just learned, but notice how the pattern of Whole Steps and Half Steps is the same.

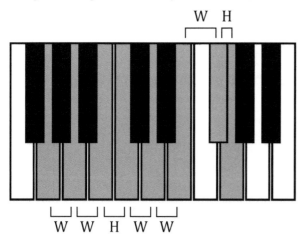

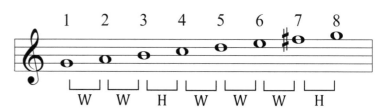

To maintain the pattern of Whole & Half Steps, the G Major Scale uses the note, F-sharp. When a piece is written with the G Major Scale as its tonal center, all of the F's are played as F-sharps. Rather than having to write the sharp every time, there's an easier way to do this, which we'll discuss below.

Keys and Key Signatures

Simply put, the KEY is the scale upon which a composition is based. The KEY SIGNATURE, which appears at the beginning of each line of music, tells you the Key of the composition, or the scale on which it is based. There are many Key Signatures which we'll learn, but for now, we're going to start with two, the KEY OF C MAJOR and the KEY OF G MAJOR.

KEY OF C MAJOR

The Key Signature for C Major is blank, therefore, you'll play all of notes on the white keys, unless you see an ACCIDENTAL (like a sharp sign) written before the note.

KEY OF G MAJOR

The Key of G Major has one sharp (F-sharp) in its Key Signature. This means that every time the note F appears, you will play F-sharp instead (you won't see the sharp sign written before each note.)

Playing the F♯

For the following piece, start with the basic five finger position with each thumb on Middle C. You'll be using your 5th finger on your left hand to play the F-sharp. Watch for the Eighth Notes in measures 6 and 14.

Jingle Bells

In the Key of C Major

J. Pierpont

Leger Lines

LEGER LINES are short lines added above or below the Staff. They are used to write a note that is too high or too low to be written on the Staff itself. You've already played a note which is written on a Leger Line, Middle C. We'll now learn two more Leger Line notes above the Bass Staff, D and E. You've been playing these exact same notes as written in the Treble Staff, with your right hand; on the following pages you'll play them as written in the Bass Staff, with your left hand.

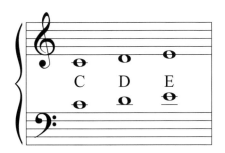

Principal Chords of G Major

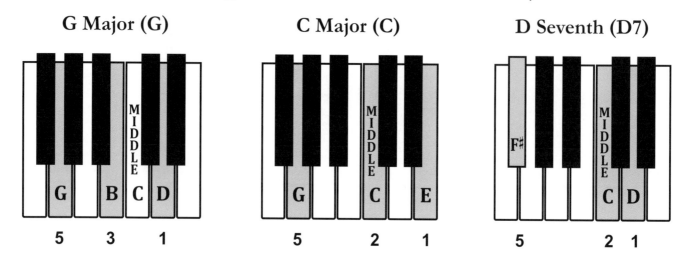

G Major (G)

C Major (C)

D Seventh (D7)

The Chords built on the first (I), fourth (IV), and fifth (V) steps of the scale are called the PRINCIPAL CHORDS of that particular Key. Earlier, you have played the Principal Chords of the Key of C Major, C (I), F(IV), and G7 (V). In the Key of G Major, the Principal Chords are G (I), C (IV), and D7 (V).

Notice that, in the Key of G Major, the C Chord (the "IV Chord") is played in a different position than what you have been used to previously. When the notes of a Chord are played in a different position as above, this is known as an INVERSION of the Chord. The three notes, however, are the same (C, E, and G).

To get used to playing these three chords, try practicing the following four chord combinations:

1. C, G, C   2. G, D7, G   3. G, C, G, D7, G   4. G, C, D7, G

The following familiar tune uses two of the Principal Chords of G Major, G and D7. The Key Signature shows one sharp, which tells you it is in the Key of G Major. This means that every time you see the note, F, you must play F-sharp. As always, it is a good idea to practice each hand separately before playing them together.

Skip to My Lou

1st and 2nd Ending Repeats

Sometimes section of music is repeated with different measures to play to the end of each pass. This is written with a FIRST & SECOND ENDING. It's very easy to play, and it saves a lot of notation space. Here's how it's done:

1. **Play the piece, including the First Ending, until you reach the Repeat Sign.**
2. **Go back to the Forward Repeat Sign and play the section again, but this time, skip over the First Ending and go directly to the Second Ending.**

Amazing Grace
CD Track 16

Did you catch everything, the Pick-up, the F-sharp, and the new Leger Line notes, and the Repeat?

New Hand Position in C Major

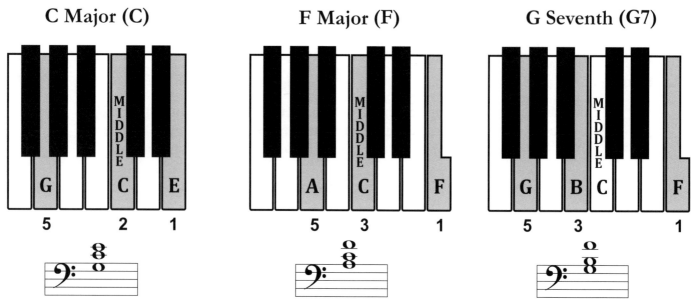

C Major (C)   **F Major (F)**   **G Seventh (G7)**

The three Chords above are different Inversions of Chords which you have already played. We're showing them on both the Keyboard and the Bass Staff, since you'll have to get used to reading the Leger Line notes above the Staff. Play each with the new hand position then practice the four Chord combinations below:

1. C, F, C   **2. C, G7, C**   **3. C, F, C, G7, C**   **4. C, F, G7, C**

The Natural Sign

♮ This is a NATURAL SIGN. It cancels a Sharp.

As you know, a Sharp in the Key Signature is usually in effect for the entire piece. It automatically changes every note of that letter name to a Sharp, without having to write the Sharp Sign before the note. A Sharp or Natural added before a note is called an ACCIDENTAL. It affects that note only, and *every note of the same letter name for the balance of the measure.* An Accidental is automatically cancelled by the Barline and the Key Signature is in full effect, once again. Sometimes, you may see an unnecessary Accidental in the following Measure. These are called CAUTIONARY ACCIDENTALS. They are added as a reminder only.

Key of G Major   **Key of C Major**   **Key of G Major**

The Natural Sign is only in effect for that measure (the barline cancels the Accidental). Play the F-sharp in the second measure per the Key Signature.

The Natural Sign in Measure #1 cancels the Sharp (Accidental) on the first note. The F-natural in the second measure is played according to the Key Signature.

The Natural Sign in Measure #1 is only in effect for that measure. The F-sharp in Measure #2 is in the Key Signature (a Cautionary Accidental is provided).

On the next few pages, we're going to give you the opportunity to play a few tunes which incorporate a lot of what you have been learning, so far. You'll have to watch for many of the elements you have seen and practiced to this point. We're not going to point out each of the different types of notes and notation, so it's really a good idea to take a look at each piece before you begin to practice. Look for things like the Key Signature, added Sharps or Naturals, Repeat Signs and Endings, Tempo, and hand position. You may also see a few surprise notes, so keep your eyes open. As always, practice each hand separately until you're able to play them reasonably well before you attempt to practice them together. Always practice slowly and build the Tempo gradually. Good Luck!

Evening Stroll

Level 1

Jonathon Robbins

Did you notice the new Chords, A7 and Dm? We'll go over those in more detail later.

Kum Ba Ya

Level 1

Traditional

As you can see from these last two examples, a 2nd Ending doesn't always occur at the end of the piece.

Down by the Riverside

CD Track 17

African American Spiritual

Did you get the rhythm correct for the dotted quarter note? We'll talk about that on the next page.

The Dotted Quarter Note

You know that the Dot adds half of the value of a note to that note. So, if the Half Note receives 2 beats, the Dotted Half Note would receive 3 beats. Augmentation Dots may be added to any note and the formula is the same each time. One rhythmic pattern you'll see often in many pieces is the DOTTED QUARTER NOTE followed by an Eighth Note. This combination creates an interesting and familiar rhythm. We have some recognizable tunes below to illustrate this, but first, let's look at the Dotted Quarter Note itself.

In 4/4 Time

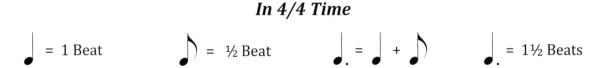

To get used to this rhythm, we have the beginnings of four tunes, which you may be familiar. Try singing the melody as you play, and you'll hear the recognizable rhythm created by the Dotted Quarter - Eighth Note combination. Then, play the tune and count the beats out loud, so you can where these notes fall into the count for each measure. Before long, you'll see how this interesting rhythm is really quite easy to play. You'll play the last example in its entirety on the following page after you get used to the dooted rhythms below.

Sing along with the following, then Play and Count the beats outloud..

Auld Lang Syne

Silent Night

All Through the Night

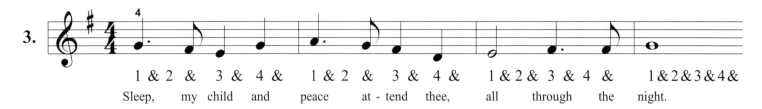

Cockles and Mussels
(Molly Malone)

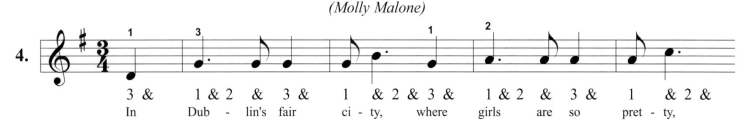

Cockles and Mussels

(Molly Malone)

CD Track 18

Moderately

Irish Folk Song

Did you notice the 2 new chords? We'll discuss some of the more advanced chords later in the book.

Broken Chords

We discussed early on that Chords may be played in two ways, as a Solid Chord in which the notes are played together, or as a Broken Chord, in which the notes are played one after the other. If we take a look below at the G Major Chord, we can see that the notes are the same, they're just played differently.

SOLID CHORD

... *becomes* ...

BROKEN CHORD

One more thing, the notes of the Broken Chord do not have to be written in any particular order and all of the notes in the Solid Chord may not be present. There are many different ways to write a Broken Chord.

Scarborough Fair
CD Track 19

English Folk Song

Congratulations! You've just completed Level 1.

Level 2

General Review

Chord Review

Observing the Rests

Common Time

The Accent

Introduction to Syncopation

The Key of F Major

Principal Chords in F Major

More Syncopation Practice

D.C. al Fine

Scale and Chord Review

The 2/4 Time Signature

The Triplet

Cut-Time

Changes in Dynamics

Introduction to Transposition

Transposing an Entire Tune

Chord Inversions

The Dominant Seventh Chord

The Waltz Pattern

Changes in Tempo

Introduction to Sight Reading

Sight Reading Chords

Phrases

Playing a 2nd Voice in One Hand

Boogie Woogie

Staccato and Legato

Johann Sebastian Bach

Ludwig van Beethoven

Choral Arrangements

General Review

Let's begin Level 2 with a quick review of some of the things you've learned. The tune below incorporates many of the concepts you are now familiar with, including a Pick-up Measure, Leger Line Notes, 1st and 2nd Ending Repeats, and both Solid and Broken Chords. As a reminder, Allegretto means moderately fast.

As always, practice each hand separately first at a slower tempo before gradually increasing the Tempo.

The Yellow Rose of Texas

CD Track 20

Traditional

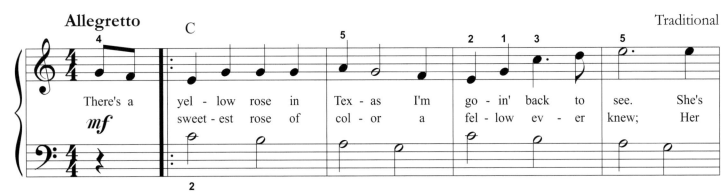

There's a yel - low rose in Tex - as I'm go - in' back to see. She's
sweet - est rose of col - or a fel - low ev - er knew; Her

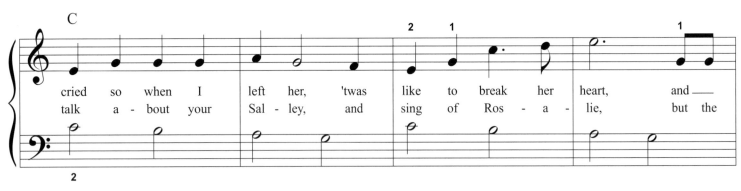

wait - ing there in Tex - as, for me, and on - ly me. She ___
eyes are bright as dia - monds. They spar - kle like the dew. You may

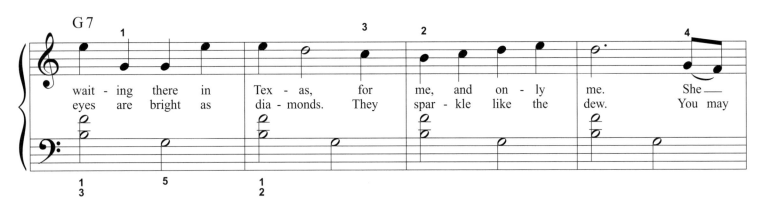

cried so when I left her, 'twas like to break her heart, and ___
talk a - bout your Sal - ley, and sing of Ros - a - lie, but the

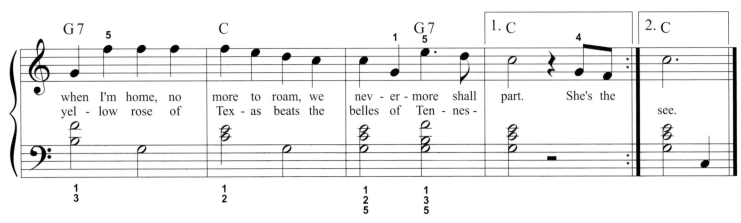

when I'm home, no more to roam, we nev - er - more shall part. She's the
yel - low rose of Tex - as beats the belles of Ten - nes - see.

Chord Review

In Level 1, we learned about Principal Chords. You'll remember that the Principal Chords in any Key are the Chords built on the 1st, 4th, and 5th notes, or DEGREES of the Scale. It is common to refer to these Chords using the Roman Numerals, I, IV, and V (pronouced, "The One Chord," "The Four Chord," and "The Five Chord"). If the Chord is a Seventh Chord, we simply add the number 7, as in "V7" (pronounced, "The Five-Seven Chord"). To identify these CHords, a system called, CHORD ANALYSIS may be used.

CHORD ANALYSIS may appear below the staff. It begins with the letter name of the Key, followed by a colon, then the Roman Numerals under each of the Chords. Take a look below and this will become much clearer.

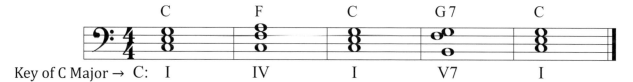

Review of the Principal Chords of C Major

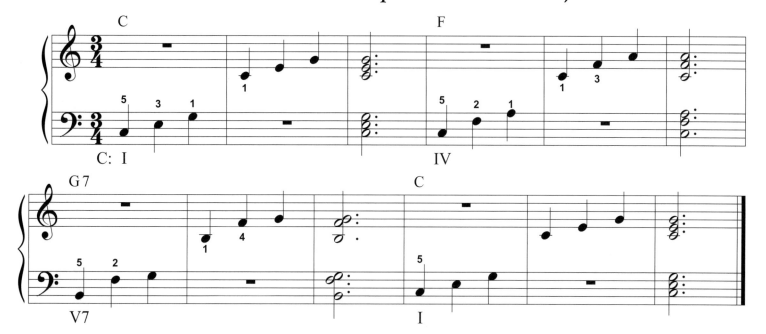

Review of the Principal Chords of G Major

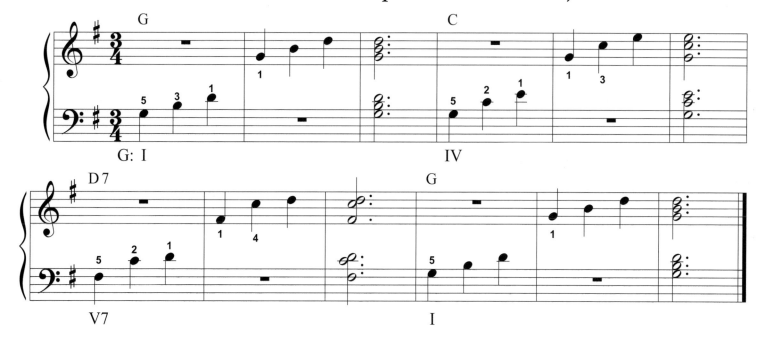

Observing the Rests

The Rests are just as important as the Notes! When a Rest is written following a Note or Chord, be sure to hold the notes for only as long as the note value itself, then lift your hand, to give the Rests their full value.

Chiapanecas

Brightly

Mexican Folk Dance

counter melody:

ff
(very loud)

Common Time

The Time Signature, COMMON TIME, is notated with the symbol, $\mathbf{C}$. It is an abbreviation for 4/4 Time.

$$\mathbf{C} \; = \; \frac{4}{4}$$

The tune below contains long slurred phrases. Be sure to play them smoothly and connected.

Red River Valley

Traditional Folk Song

The Accent

➤ This is an ACCENT (in Italian, "Marcato"). It tells you to give the Note or Chord additional emphasis.

The Accent (Marcato) is part of a group of musical symbols called ARTICULATIONS. These symbols direct you to play the notes they're attached to in a certain way. You'll be introduced to more of them as you progress. When you play an accented note, give it additional emphasis, but don't strike it too hard.

Camptown Races
CD Track 21

Stephen Foster

If you played the Accented notes correctly, they should stand out a little more than the non-accented notes.

Introduction to Syncopation

Generally, the first beat of each measure receives a slight, natural emphasis. It's not as much as an accented note, but it should be noticable. In 4/4 Time, it is natural to give the first beat of each measure this natural emphasis and then to give the third beat a smaller, natural emphasis. Imagine the size of the numbers below as an idication of how strong each of the four beats in the measure would be, and they would look like this:

$$\frac{4}{4} \Big| \quad \mathbf{1} \quad 2 \quad \mathbf{3} \quad 4 \Big| \quad \mathbf{1} \quad 2 \quad \mathbf{3} \quad 4 \Big| \quad \mathbf{1} \quad 2 \quad \mathbf{3} \quad 4$$

SYNCOPATION is a variation in the rhythm in a way which is unexpected. It places the rhymthic stresses in places that they usually don't naturally occur. While this can be accomplished using Articulations, more often than not, a Syncopated Rhythm is created using dotted notes and tied notes, so that the notes are attacked on what is known as the OFF-BEAT. Syncopated Rhythms are very popular in many different musical styles.

The study below may be the most challenging you've attempted, so far. The count for each beat is written in every measure. The left hand part will provide a steady beat, as the right hand plays various Syncopated Rhythms. Practice slowly and count each half beat out loud. At first, the two parts may appear to "work" against each other, but once you get a good feel for this type of rhythm, you'll find it sounds very interesting.

Syncopation Study

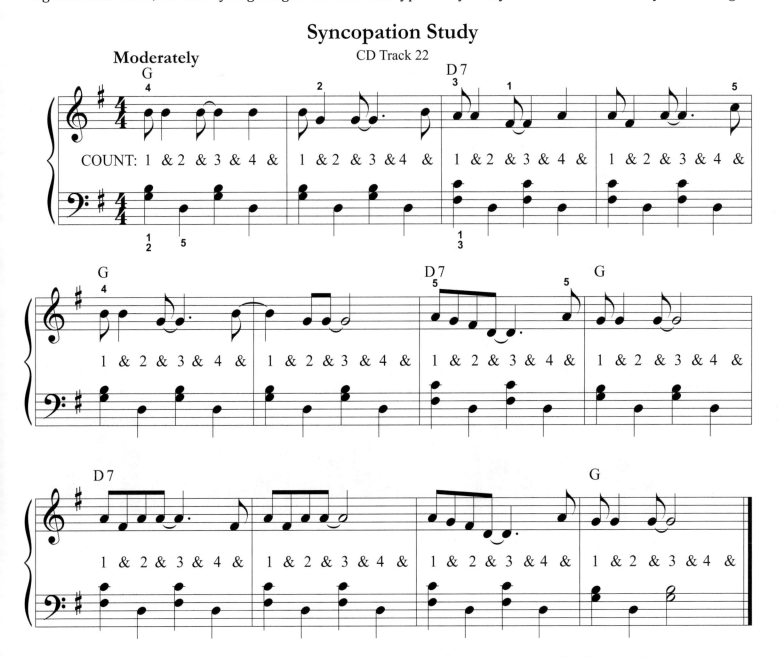

Syncopated Rhythms are common in many types of popular music, including Jazz and Ragtime.

The Key of F Major

The Flat Sign

 This is a FLAT sign. When you see it before a note on the Staff, like this ...

... play that note one Half Step lower. This note is pronounced, "B-flat."

Think of a Flat as very much like a Sharp, but in the other direction. Here's what is looks like on the keyboard.

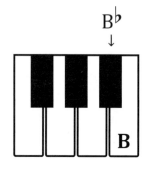

You know that a Half Step is the distance between any two touching keys on the piano, therefore, to play the note, B-flat, find any B on the keyboard and play the black note directly to the left, which lowers the note by one Half Step. Find all of the B-flats on the piano now.

The F Major Scale

Since a Major Scale may begin on any note, to construct the F Major scale, we just have to make sure that we adhere to the strict pattern of Whole Steps and Half Steps which every Major Scale must have.

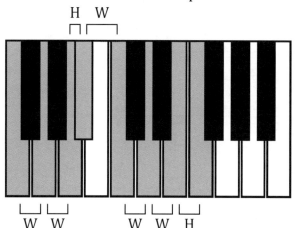

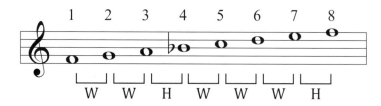

So, by adding the note, B-flat, we can construct an F Major Scale with the necessary pattern of Whole Steps and Half Steps, therefore, the Key Signature for F Major contains one Flat.

Review of the Natural Sign

We discussed earlier that the Natural Sign (♮) cancels a Sharp. It also cancels a Flat. The same rules apply with Sharps and Flats when either written in the Key Signature, or added as an Accidental before the note.

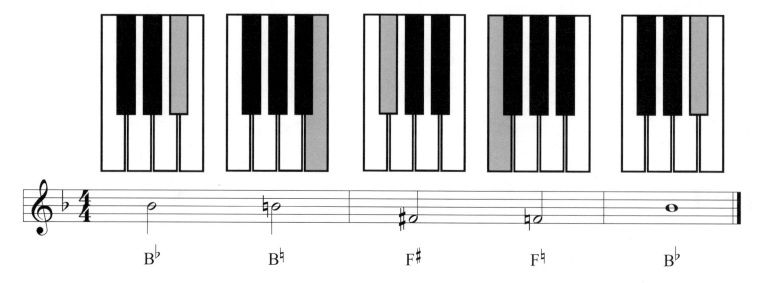

Principal Chords of F Major

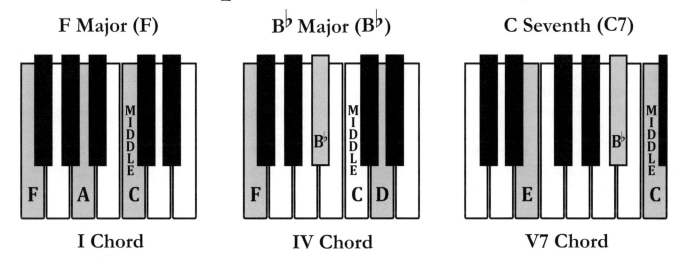

F Major (F)   **B♭ Major (B♭)**   **C Seventh (C7)**

I Chord   IV Chord   V7 Chord

To get used to playing these three chords, try practicing the following four chord combinations:

1. F, B♭, F   2. F, C7, F   3. F, B♭, F, C7, F   4. F, B♭, C7, F

Good-Night, Ladies

(in the Key of F Major)

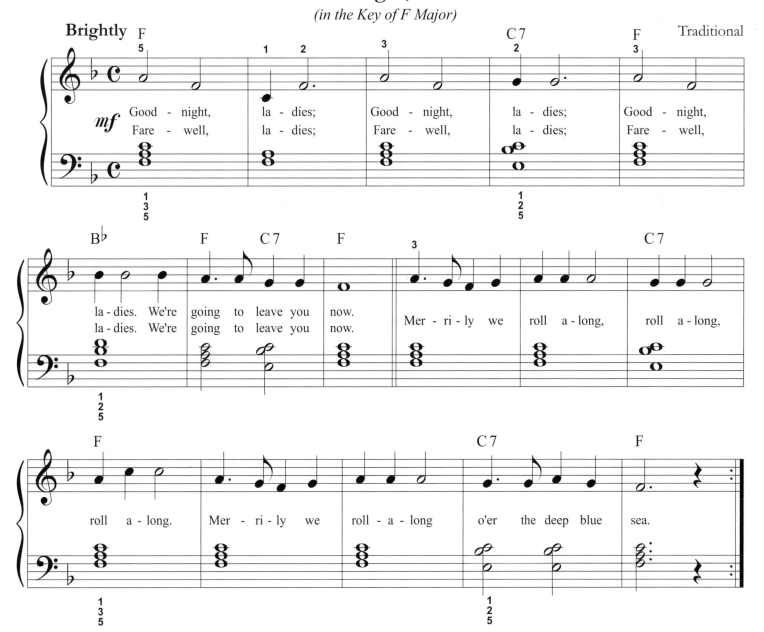

- 45 -

More Syncopation Practice

Here's a Syncopated tune that you're sure to recognize. The left hand has been written in a steady rhythm to help you keep the beat, while the right hand plays the Syncopated melody. There are also two surprises. There are three endings on the repeat. Play the repeated section with the ending marked, "1., 2." twice, then proceed to the 3rd ending on the next pass. There is also a new chord just to make the accompaniment interesting. We won't go over Diminished Chords just yet, but listen to how nicely it leads up to the C7 Chord.

He's Got the Whole World in His Hands

CD Track 23

Traditional Spiritual

D.C. al Fine

Sometimes, it will be necessary to repeat a passage in a tune from the beginning, but to end the piece before reaching the last measure a second time. This type of repeat is notated using the **D.C al Fine** repeat. The abbreviation, D.C. is from the Italian, "Da Capo," meaning, "From the Head," and the Italian word, "Fine" (pronounced, "fee-nay"), means the "End." So, this Italian phrase literally means, "From the Head to the End." When you reach the **D.C. al Fine**, return to the beginning and stop when you see the word, **Fine**. (Don't stop at the word "Fine" the first time through, however). There are also two pick-up measures and two partial measures. This is because the piece is divided into two sections and the music must always add up mathematically to form complete measures. You'll also notice that there is no final double barline.

Swing Low, Sweet Chariot

CD Track 24

Traditional Spiritual

This is a good example of a piece with more than one Pick-up Measure.

Scale and Chord Review

Key of C Major
Principal Chords: I (C) - IV (F) - V7 (G7)

Key of G Major
Principal Chords: I (G) - IV (C) - V7 (D7)

Key of F Major
Principal Chords: I (F) - IV (B♭) - V7 (C7)

The 2/4 Time Signature

You already know the rules for Time Signatures, so 2/4 Time is very similar to those you have learned, so far.

2/4 There are 2 Beats in each Measure
The Quarter Note receives one Beat

Au Clair de la Lune

French Folk Song

The G7 Chord is not one of the Principal Chords in F Major, but it leads nicely into the C7 Chord.

The Triplet

 The TRIPLET is a grouping of three notes which occupy the same number of beats which two notes would normally occupy. Any type of note may be grouped into a Triplet, but one of the most common is the EIGHTH NOTE TRIPLET.

In this case, three Eighth Notes occupy the same space as two. The Triplet is identified by the number, "3" written above or below the group of three notes. In the case of the Eighth Note Triplet, assuming the Quarter Note receives one beat, each of the Eighth Notes in the Triplet would receive one-third of a beat. That's not as complicated as it might sound. It just means that the beat is equally divided into three parts. Count the beats comprised of the Triplet in this way: 1 & a, 2 & a.

This challenging Jig uses the **D.S. al Fine Repeat** (Dal Segno al Fine). It's similar to the **D.C al Fine**, except instead of going back to the beginning, return to the measure with the Segno (Sign), which looks like this: 𝄋

The Irish Washerwoman

CD Track 25

Traditional Irish

Cut-Time

Common Time

Cut-Time

If you look at each example above, you may be thinking, "They look the same." In many ways, you would be correct. The measures written in Cut-Time do look just like those in Common Time. There appears to be the same number of beats in each measure, with the same types of notes receiving the same number of beats. Cut-Time is generally used for faster pieces with a strong feeling of two beats in each measure. Quick Marches, for example, are generally written in Cut-Time, but what exactly does Cut-Time mean?

$$\mathbf{C} = \frac{4}{4} \qquad \mathbf{\mathcal{C}} = \frac{2}{2}$$

In Common Time, which you also know as 4/4 Time, there are 4 Beats in each Measure, with the Quarter Note receiving 1 Beat. Now, let's cut those numbers in half. In Cut-Time (which is the equivalent of 2/2 Time), there are only 2 Beats in each Measure and the Half Note receives 1 Beat. This makes it much easier to read in faster tempos without having to count at a very quick pace and use much smaller note values. By the way, while you may see Common Time written as 4/4 Time often, you'll almost never see Cut-Time written as 2/2 Time in the Time Signature. You can count Cut-Time as 1-2-3-4 when you're practicing at a slow tempo.

Technically speaking, though, the note values in Cut-Time are as follows:

o = 2 Beats   𝅗𝅥 = 1 Beat   𝅘𝅥 = ½ Beat   𝅘𝅥𝅮 = ¼ Beat

Cut-Time Exercise

The following exercise contains a more difficult left hand bass pattern.
It's very common in many popular and jazz tunes, dances. and marches.

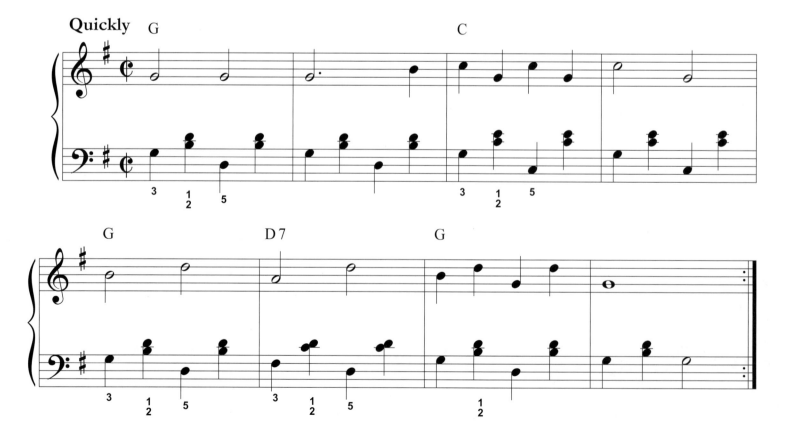

Changes in Dynamics

Crescendo - Play Louder

cresc.

Diminuendo - Play Softer

dim. or *decresc.*

The symbols and text for CRESCENDO and DIMINUENDO (or, Decrescendo) direct you to gradually increase or decrease the volume while playing. They generally appear between the Treble and Bass Staff.

The Key of D Major

Here's a new Key - D Major. It has two sharps in its Key Signature.

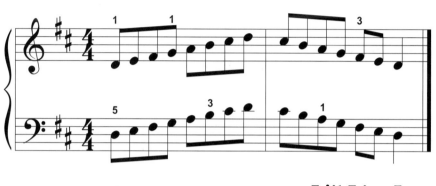

L'il Liza Jane

CD Track 26

Traditional

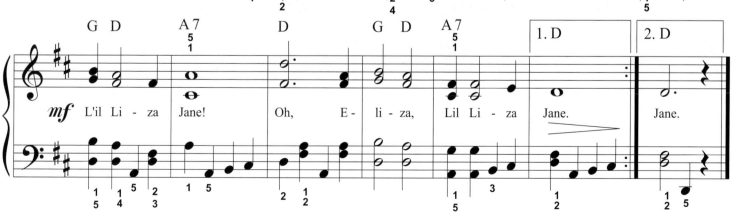

Introduction to Transposition

TRANSPOSITION is the process of changing the key of a piece of music, that is changing the melody to a higher or lower pitch, while keeping the relationships between the notes the same. We should let you know that learning to transpose a melody while playing is a relatively advanced skill, so don't expect to master this technique quickly. It's useful, though, to be familiar with at least the basics of transposing while playing.

You may wonder why it would be necessary to learn to Transpose a piece of music which somebody has already written in a particluar key. The fact is you may not need to Transpose often or at all, but if you would like to play along with a vocalist, it is very common that the music is written either too high or too low for the range of the singer. In this case, you'll need to be able to Transpose the melody to the vocalist's preferred key.

There's no shortcut to learning this valuable skill. It takes quite a bit of practice, but there are some things you can learn quickly which will allow you to look for the key elements in a melody as you learn to Transpose.

Take a look a the first line of the tune, ***Camptown Races***, in the Key of G Major, then transposed to C Major.

Let's say that the original melody in the Key of C Major is too low for your vocalist, so you've been asked to Transpose it up to the Key of G Major. If we look at the original melody, here's what we know right away:

1. **The melody begins on the 5th Note (5th Degree) of the C Major Scale.**
2. **The melody begins with the I Chord (C), then switches to the V7 Chord (G7).**
3. **There are no added Accidentals in the melody. All notes are in the Key Signature.**

So, to Transpose to the Key of G Major, we know we have to start on the 5th Note or Degree of the G Major Scale, which is the note, D. We also know that the first Chord will be the I Chord, or the G Chord in our new key, and the new V7 Chord will be the D7 Chord. We can even copy the hand position from the old key and play the original pattern in the new key. Yes, there is a lot more you'll need to practice to learn this technique, but these are simple steps that anyone can do, and they're a good place to start learning this process.

Let's jump right in and try to Transpose the first line of the tune, ***Mary Ann***,
from the Key of F Major ***up one step*** to the Key of G Major.

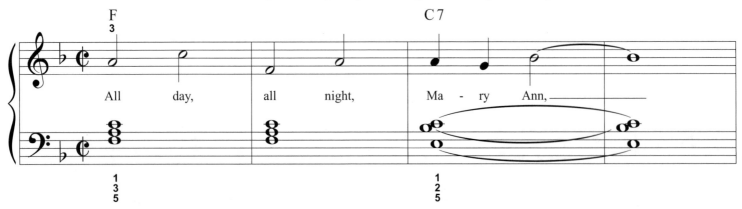

Transposing an Entire Tune

Now you're going to attempt to transpose the entire tune. Don't rush through this process, instead, take your time and think. Keep the relationship between the notes, hand position, and the chord analysis in mind as you play through the first time in the Key of F Major. After you learn the tune well, you'll attempt to transpose the entire tune into two different keys, the Key of G Major and the Key of C Major.

Play the tune, **Mary Ann**:

1. As written below in the Key of F Major.
2. Transposed up to the Key of G Major.
3. Transposed down to the Key of C Major.

Mary Ann
Hint: There are only 2 Chords in this tune, the I Chord (F) and the V7 Chord (C7)

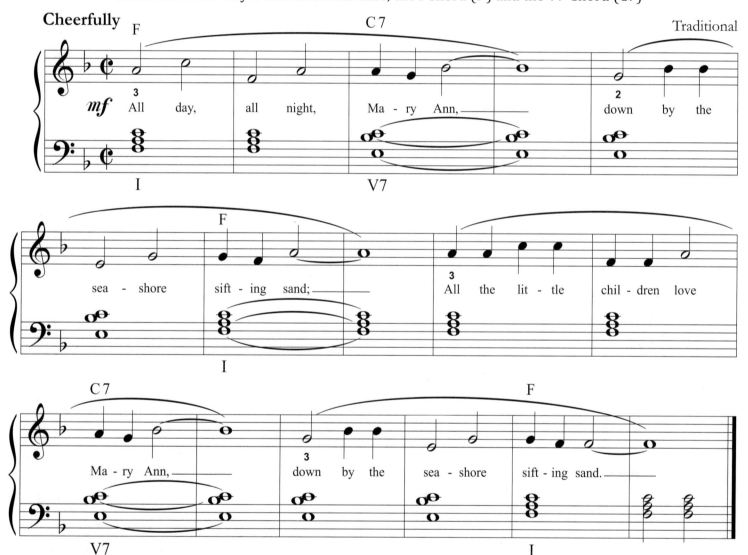

Did you get your Chords right? The I Chord in the Key of G Major is G, and in the Key of C Major it's C, while the V7 Chord is D7 in the Key of G Major and G7 in the Key of C Major.

The best way to learn to Transpose well is to keep practicing it repeatedly with very simple tunes. Try the following melodies which you have already played in this method. Transpose the following from ...

C Major to F Major	C Major to G Major	G Major to F Major	G Major to C Major
"Ode to Joy"	"Lightly Row"	"Kum Ba Ya"	"Skip to My Lou"
"Jingle Bells"	"Little Piece"	"Amazing Grace"	"Camptown Races"

Hint: Tunes with simple chords make the best choices when you're learning to Transpose.

Chord Inversions

The word, INVERSION, means something which has be turned upside down. When we Invert a chord, that is precisely what we are doing. The Chord is turned upside down by taking the bottom note and placing it on the top. This give us three different ways to play a basic 3-note chord in three different positions.

The Triad
A TRIAD is a chord composed of three notes.

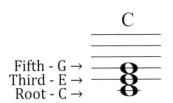

Fifth - G →
Third - E →
Root - C →

The ROOT is the note upon which the chord is built and named.
The THIRD is the third note in the scale up from the Root.
The FIFTH is the fifth note in the scale up from the Root.

Inverting the C Major Triad

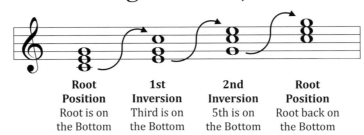

Root Position	1st Inversion	2nd Inversion	Root Position
Root is on the Bottom	Third is on the Bottom	5th is on the Bottom	Root back on the Bottom

C Major Triad Inversion Exercise

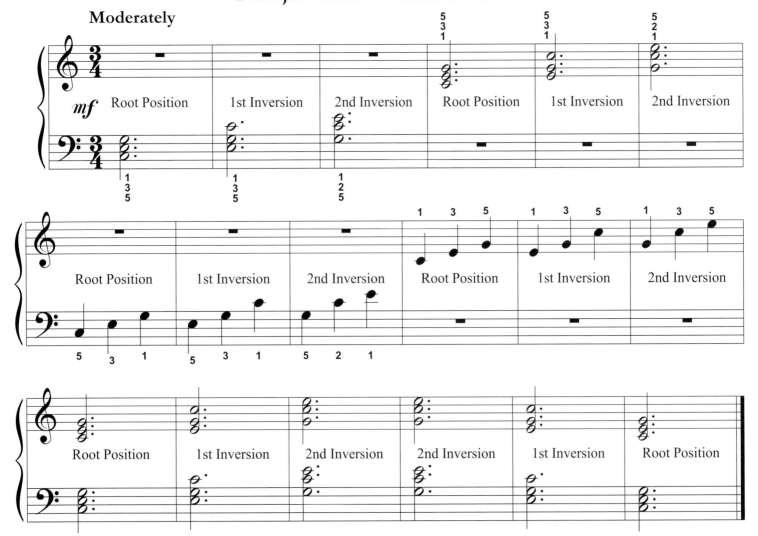

After you have mastered this exercise in the Key of C, transpose it to the Key of F and to the Key of G.

The Dominant Seventh Chord

As you have learned, the Principal Chords of a Key are built on the 1st, 4th, and 5th notes, or Degrees, of the scale of that Key. These are the most important Chords for harmonizing melodies in any key. You also know these Chords as the I Chord, the IV Chord, and the V7 Chord. To review, these Principal Chords are:

In the Key of C Major ... C (I) - F (IV) - G7 (V7)

In the Key of G Major ... G (I) - C (IV) - D7 (V7)

In the Key of F Major ... F (I) - B♭ (IV) - C7 (V7)

Each of these Degrees of the Scale and the Chords built upon them have special names:

I - the TONIC
IV - the SUB-DOMINANT
V - the DOMINANT

THE TONIC CHORD is a Triad built on the First Degree (The Tonic) of the scale. It contains a Root, 3rd, and 5th, and the letter names of the notes in the Chord skip one letter in between each note, as in C - E - G, which is the Tonic Triad in the Key of C Major.

THE SUB-DOMINANT CHORD is a Triad built on the Fourth Degree (The Sub-Dominant) of the scale. It also contains a Root, 3rd, and 5th and the letter names of the notes in this Chord also skip one letter in between each of the notes. The notes F - A - C make up the Sub-Dominant Triad in the Key of C Major.

THE DOMINANT CHORD can be a Triad (you know that a Triad may be built on any note), but the Chord you know as the V7 Chord is not a Triad. You may have noticed that while the V7 Chords you have been playing do contain just three notes, they aren't arranged in the same way that the I and IV are built. They don't skip a letter name in between all of the notes. This is because you have been playing a variety of the DOMINANT SEVENTH CHORD, which is not a Triad at all. It is a SEVENTH CHORD, built with 4 notes (the Root, 3rd, 5th, and 7th). The COMPLETE DOMINANT SEVENTH CHORD does contain 4 notes which each skip a letter name.

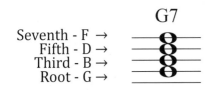

Seventh - F →
Fifth - D →
Third - B →
Root - G →

As you can see, when all 4 notes are present, the SEVENTH CHORD appears to be built exactly the same as a Triad with the addition of one more note. When it is built on the 5th Degree of the scale (the Dominant), it becomes the DOMINANT SEVENTH CHORD. Now, let's practice playing Seventh Chords.

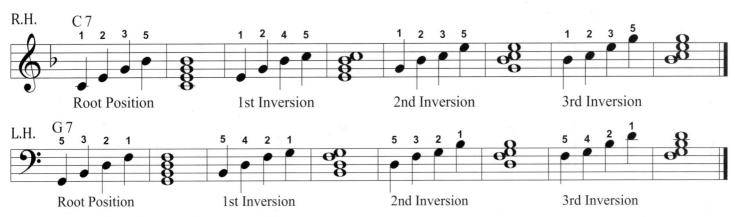

One last thing, although the Seventh Chord is a 4-note chord, it is very common to see it played as a 3-note chord. This does not mean that it is a Triad. It is still a Seventh Chord, but when it contains only 3 of the 4 notes, it is known as an INCOMPLETE DOMINANT SEVENTH CHORD. Generally, you'll see an Incomplete Dominant Seventh Chord with the 5th omitted. The Root, 3rd, and 7th are the most important tones.

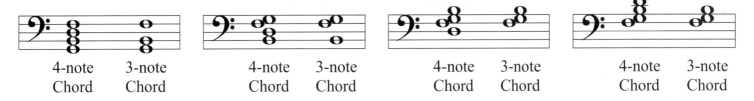

| 4-note Chord | 3-note Chord | 4-note Chord | 3-note Chord | 4-note Chord | 3-note Chord | 4-note Chord | 3-note Chord |

The Waltz Pattern

The WALTZ is a traditional dance with three beats in each measure, usually written in 3/4 Time. The Bass Pattern in most Waltzes consists of a bass note followed by two chords, as in the example below.

The Waltz often uses a Bass Pattern known as the ALTERNATE BASS. This type of bass generally consists of the Root and the Third or Fifth as the Alternating Bass Notes on the first beat of each measure. This creates a strong sense of the first beat while adding variety and a sense of movement to the Bass Pattern.

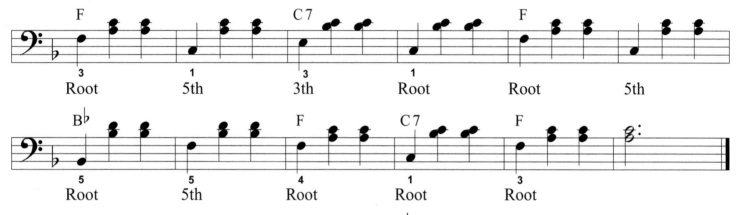

The Key of B♭ Major

This next piece will introduce a new key, the Key of B♭ Major.
Notice that there are two flats in the Key Signature, B♭ and E♭.

Clementine

Remember to keep the Key Signature in mind. You'll be able to hear if you miss a flat!

F. Montrose

Changes in Tempo

There are several musical terms which indicate gradual changes in Tempo (speed). We'll start with these two:

Ritardando - Gradually slow down
Abbreviation - *ritard.* or *rit.*

Accelerando - Gradually speed up
Abbreviation - *accel.*

There are also two new symbols in the piece below. The FERMATA ($\frown$) instructs you to hold the note or chord for longer than its normal duration, and the dymanic marking, PIANISSIMO (*pp*) means very soft.

On Top of Old Smoky
CD Track 27

- 59 -

Introduction to Sight Reading

SIGHT READING is the ability to play a piece of music reasonably well the first time you see it. Like the skill of Transposition, Sight Reading requires a lot of practice. While playing the piano does not necessarily require you to Sight Read well, if you want to be able to play along with other musicians, and certainly if you aspire to play professionally, then the ability to Sight Read is not only important, but essential.

Like Transposing, Sight Reading requires that you take a quick look at the music and "take inventory" of the things which will make it easier for you to navigate through the tune. These things include elements such as the Time Signature and Key Signature, but also a general overview of the rhythmic patterns.

Sight Reading boils down to doing two things, reading notes and reading rhythms. If you continue to practice reading the melody of many different tunes, in time you'll become proficient at reading notes at sight. Reading rhythms requires you to take notice of certain patterns. Let's look at this aspect a little more closely.

Reading Rhythms

Practice the following rhythms. Take note of the Time Signature, then watch for similar rhythmic patterns.

4/4 Rhythm Patterns

3/4 Rhythm Patterns

Sight Reading Chords

Now let's combine Sight Reading rhythms with Sight Reading chords. You are familiar with many chords written in Root Position and various Inversions. You have played Triads and Seventh Chords and have a pretty good idea of what they look like and the names of these chords, as well. Use that experience when attempting to Sight Read chords. Consider the names of the chords from the chord symbols, recognize when chords are repeated and when they change, and whether the chord is a Triad or a Seventh Chord. Combine this with reading the rhythms and you'll have a good head start towards learning to Sight Read.

Practice Sight Reading the following chord and rhythmic patterns. Don't stop if you make a mistake. Unlike practicing a specific piece for performance, when Sight Reading, you must keep playing and fix mistakes the next time through. Maintain a strict tempo as you attempt to recognize familiar rhythmic patterns and notes.

Sight Reading Chords in 4/4 Time

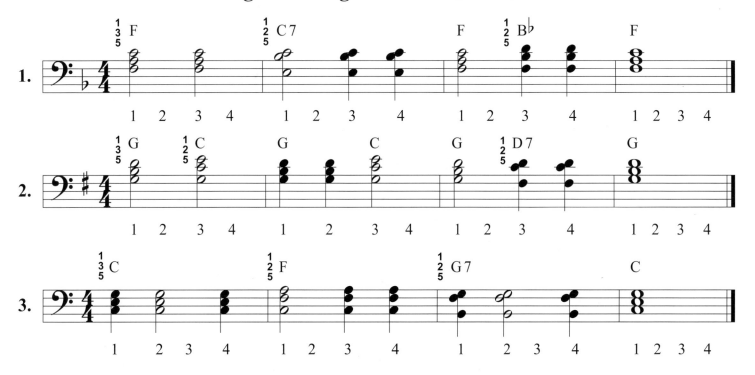

Sight Reading Chords in 3/4 Time

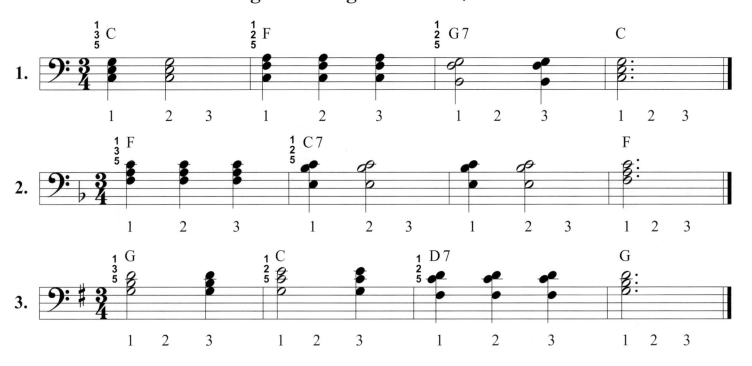

Phrases

In piano music, when a Slur appears over two or more notes, this is referred to as a PHRASE. A Phrase is like a musical sentence. The notes of the phrase should be played smoothly and when the phrase ends, you should be able to hear a slight separation before the next note. Think of phrases like lines of poetry which, when put together, make up the entire poem. It's the same in music. Phrases combine to form an entire piece. When practicing phrasing, lift slightly after the last note in a phrase before attacking the next note.

We Wish You a Merry Christmas

There are some new chords in the above tune. We'll cover some of these advanced chords later.

Playing a 2nd Voice in One Hand

Notice in several measures below (measures 9, 10, 15, and 16), there appears to be another line of music on the Treble Staff. There is a Second Voice to be played with the same hand. The piano is unique, in that we have five independent fingers on each hand, therefore, one finger may be holding a note of a longer value, while others are playing additional notes at the same time. In these measures below, you'll hold the lower note with the suggested finger, while you play the upper line of notes with your other fingers, as indicated.

Deck the Halls
In the Key of D Major

Traditional Welsh

Boogie Woogie

BOOGIE WOOGIE is a musical style which became popular in the 1920s. It is believed that its roots are from the African American communities from the late 1800s. Boogie Woogie is based on the traditional I-IV-V chord progression typical in the Blues, but it is generally faster and mainly associated with dancing. To play the characteristic bass line in Boogie Woogie, give the first eighth note in each beat a slight emphasis. You should be able to hear the "1-2-3-4" count in the bass line. Boogie Woogie, like Blues, usually has a twelve measure (or Twelve Bar) repeating pattern, with the same chord progression repeating over and over again.

Boogie Woogie Exercise

Boogie in C
Repeat these 12 Bars as many times as you wish

Tip: When you are comfortable, try transposing this Boogie to the Keys of F Major and G Major.

Staccato and Legato

STACCATO is an Italian term meaning detached or disconnected. In music, it is notated with a dot above or below the note, usually on the Note Head side. It tells you to play the note with a shortened duration. It is very important to understand that Staccato does not mean to attack the note any differently; it means to release the note sooner than expected. The opposite of Staccato is LEGATO, meaning, "tied together." This may be indicated by a Slur or with the term, *legato*, written above or below the notes. As you've learned, Legato passages should be played smoothly and connected.

Staccato Study
CD Track 28

 A two-note phrase with a Staccato on the second note is played with a Down-Up motion, down on the first note, then up with the wrist when releasing the second note.

Merry Minuet
CD Track 29

Did you remember to lift at the end of each phrase which ends with a Staccato Note?

Johann Sebastian Bach

Johann Sebastian Bach was a composer of the BAROQUE PERIOD. Born into a musical family in 1685, he became a master of counterpoint creating well known compositions such as "Toccata and Fugue in D Minor," the "Mass in B Minor," the "Brandenburg Concertos," and "The Well-Tempered Clavier" (a collection of 24 Preludes and Fugues considered part of the standard literature for all piano students). The Minuet below is from the *Notebook for Anna Magdalena Bach*, a collection of short pieces Bach presented to his second wife.

Minuet

Johann Sebastian Bach

Ludwig van Beethoven

Ludwig van Beethoven was a German composer and pianist of the CLASSICAL and ROMANTIC PERIODS. He is considered to be a crucial figure in defining the transition between these two important musical eras. The basic 4-note theme from his Symphony No. 5 is perhaps the best known and universally recognizable theme in all of classical music. By 1800 his hearing began to deteriorate, and by the last decade of his life, he was nearly totally deaf. Amazingly, some of his most admired works came from this period of his life.

Russian Folk Song

Ludwig van Beethoven

Choral Arrangements

CHORAL STYLE is written for the four vocal ranges found in a Choir: Soprano, Alto, Tenor, and Bass, with four distinct lines of music. The Soprano and Alto parts are usually written on the Treble Staff and the Tenor and Bass parts on the Bass Staff. The higher part is written with stems up, and the lower part with stems down, no matter where the notes happen to fall on the staff. Single notes with two stems are sung by both parts.

We conclude Level 2 with this Choral Arrangement of a familiar classic. The fingerings are challenging and you won't be familiar with many of the chords below, but listen to the rich harmonies as you play them.

America the Beautiful

CD Track 30

Katherine Lee Bates

Level 3

Coordination Study

Alberti Bass

Intervals

The 6/8 Time Signature

The Key of E♭ Major

Playing Melodies with the Left Hand

Introducing the Pedals

Practicing with the Sustain Pedal

Major and Minor Thirds

Rock Style

The Blues

The Coda

More About 6/8 Time

The Rhumba Rhythm

The Medley

Types of Triads

Arpeggios

Ragtime

The Relative Minor

Playing the Harmonic Minor Form

The Sixteenth Note

The Dotted Eighth Note

Wolfgang Amadeus Mozart

Modulation

Counting 6/8 Time in "Two"

Advanced Syncopation

Common Major Scales

Common Harmonic Minor Scales

Arpeggio & Chord Reference Guide

Coordination Study

Charles-Louis Hanon was a French piano teacher and composer. He is best known for his work, **The Virtuoso Pianist in 60 Exercises**, which is by far, the most widely used collection of exercises for piano used today. The Russian composer, Sergei Rachmaninoff claimed Hanon's works to be the secret to why Russian schools produced so many virtuoso pianists. The exercise below is an adaptation of Hanon's first exercise in the collection. Play it slowly and evenly, concentrating on keeping each hand perfectly syncronized, then gradually increase the tempo until you can play it rapidly, but most importantly, accurately and evenly. You'll see some new notes below the Bass Staff, the low C and the low B, which use two leger lines below the staff.

CD Track 31

C. L. Hanon

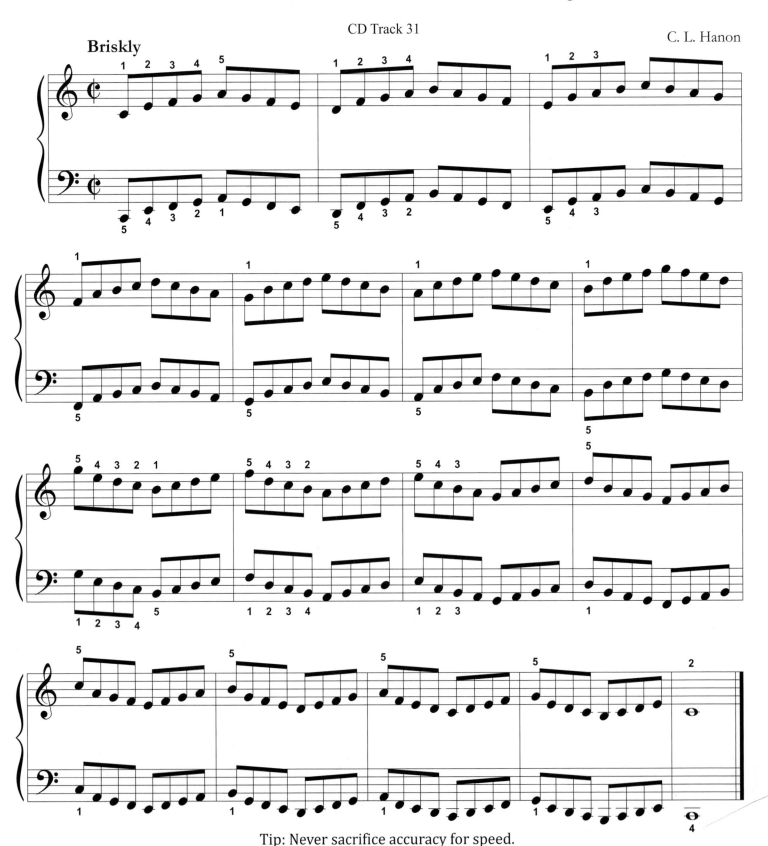

Tip: Never sacrifice accuracy for speed.

Alberti Bass

ALBERTI BASS is an accompaniment pattern which was very common in the Classical Era. It is named after Domenico Alberti, who lived during the early 1700s and used this pattern extensively. Alberti Bass is a broken chord accompaniment whose notes are played in the order of lowest, highest, middle, highest.

SOLID CHORD   ALBERTI BASS

Michael, Row the Boat Ashore

Moderately Slow   Traditional Spiritual

mf
1. Mi - chael, row the boat a - shore, Hal - le - lu -
3. Trum - pet sound the ju - bi - lee, Hal - le - lu -

Alberti Bass:

jah! Mi - chael, row the boat a - shore, Hal - le - lu - jah!
jah! Trum - pet sound the ju - bi - lee, Hal - le - lu - jah!

Fine

2. Sis - ter help to trim the sails, Hal - le - lu -

Counter Melody:

jah! Sis - ter help to trim the sails, Ha - le - lu - jah!

D.C. al Fine

Intervals

An INTERVAL is the distance between two notes.
Intervals are named using numbers, as in the Interval of a 2nd, 3rd, 4th, 5th, 6th, or 7th.

To calculate an Interval, count the total number of letter names from the first note to the second, including the two notes themselves. Always count up the alphabet. Take a look at the following examples:

C to D: Includes two letter names, therefore, the Interval is a 2nd.
D to F: Includes three letter names, therefore, the Interval is a 3rd.
A to G: Includes seven letter names, therefore, the Interval is a 7th.

Here are some examples of a few Intervals as seen on the Staff:

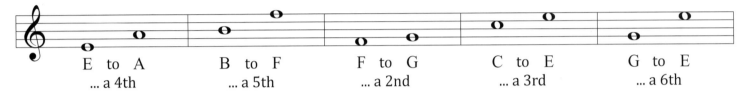

E to A	B to F	F to G	C to E	G to E
... a 4th	... a 5th	... a 2nd	... a 3rd	... a 6th

An Interval which appears in a melody line, that is, one note following another, is called a MELODIC INTERVAL.

An Interval between two notes played at the same time, as in a chord, is called a HARMONIC INTERVAL.

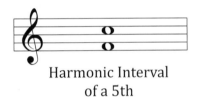

Melodic Interval
of a 5th

Harmonic Interval
of a 5th

Harmonic Interval Exercises

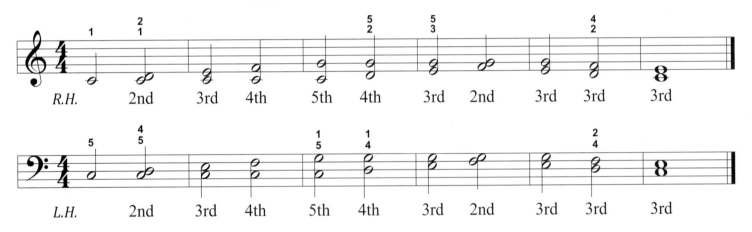

Melodic Interval Exercises

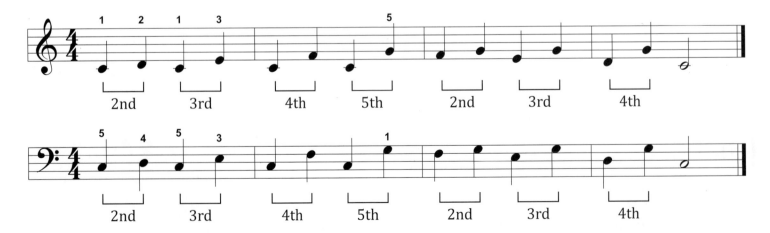

The 6/8 Time Signature

There are 6 Beats in each Measure
The Eighth Note receives one Beat

The note values in 6/8 Time are as follows:

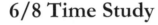
♪ = 1 Beat   ♩ = 2 Beats   ♩. = 3 Beats   𝅗𝅥. = 6 Beats

In 6/8 Time, the first beat in each measure receives a natural emphasis and the third beat receives a smaller, natural emphasis. This gives a strong sense of the measure being divided into two parts. In fact, at faster tempos, it is common to count 6/8 Time as if there were only two beats in each measure. You'll probably notice this "two beat" feel right away, but you should count six beats for now, until you get used to this Time Signature.

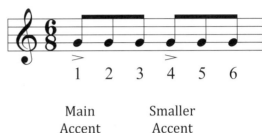

Main Accent   Smaller Accent

Because of this strong feeling of "two," eighth notes in 6/8 Time are beamed in groups of three. Between beats 3 and 4, there is an IMAGINARY BARLINE dividing the measure into two parts. A note should never cross this imaginary line, with the exception of the dotted half note, which would occupy the entire measure. All other notes being held over the Imaginary Barline would be notated with two notes tied together.

6/8 Time Study

The Farmer in the Dell

CD Track 32   Traditional

The Key of E♭ Major

The Key of E♭ Major has three flats in its Key Signature, B♭, E♭, and A♭.

Principal Chord Exercise in the Key of E♭ Major

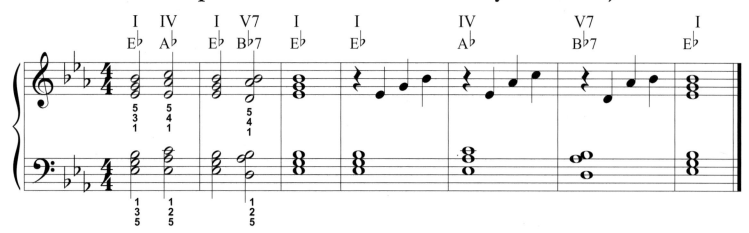

For He's a Jolly Good Fellow

CD Track 33

Traditional

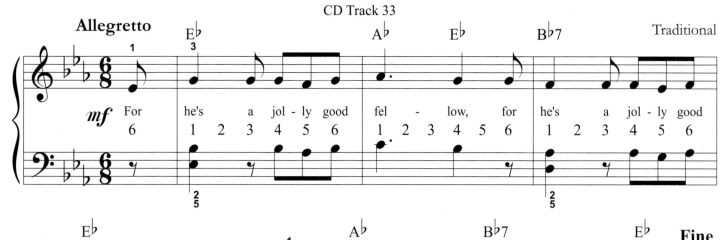

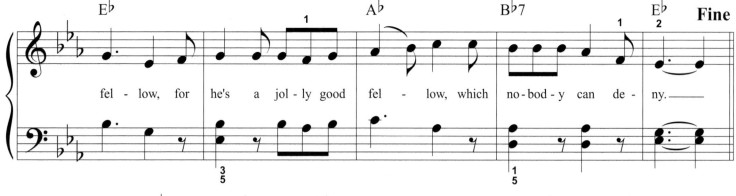

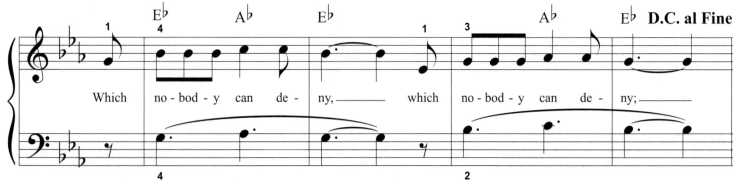

Have you noticed that the groups of 3 beamed eighth notes in 6/8 Time have a "triplet" feel?

Playing Melodies with the Left Hand Level 3

So far, you've been playing pieces with the melody in the right hand and the accompaniment in the left hand. There are many compositions, however, in which these roles are reversed. Sometimes, the melody will switch to the bass staff and you'll play it with your left hand. When this occurs, play the right hand accompaniment a little softer and the left hand melody a little louder. At first, you may find it ackward to coordinate, but with a little practice, you'll soon become comfortable with switching the melody from the right to the left hand.

In the piece below, watch the phrasing and notice that the left hand is playing the melody in measures 9 - 12.

The Cuckoo

German Folk Song

Introducing the Pedals

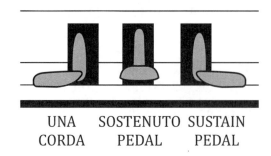

UNA   SOSTENUTO SUSTAIN
CORDA   PEDAL   PEDAL

Most Pianos have three pedals. If yours has only two, it will be missing the middle pedal, which is rarely used.

The pedal to the left is called the UNA CORDA, meaning "One Cord," or "One String." It is also commonly referred to as the SOFT PEDAL, because that is what it does. On a Grand Piano, depressing the pedal shifts the keyboard to the right, such that the HAMMERS (the parts which strike the strings) will hit one less string for the notes containing more than one string, or part of the string for the lower notes containing just the one string. This results in a softer sound. On an Upright Piano, the mechanism is a little different, but the resulting sound is the same. This pedal is operated with the left foot and would be used for notes which are already being played softly. There would be no noticable effect on notes which are played more loudly.

The Middle Pedal, known as the SOSTENUTO PEDAL, will sustain only the notes currently depressed. If you play and hold down the notes of a chord, then depress the pedal, those notes only will be sustained and any other notes played will sound as they normally would. As stated previously, this pedal is rarely used.

Finally, we come to the pedal on the right, the SUSTAIN PEDAL (sometimes referred to as the DAMPER PEDAL). This is the most often used pedal and the one we'll be discussing. DAMPERS are felt blocks which rest on or against the strings to prevent them from vibrating when they are not being played. When you strike and hold a key, two things happen at the same time, the Damper lifts away from the string and the Hammer strikes the string(s). When you release the key, the Damper returns to its position on the string(s) and stops the note from continuing to sound. When you depress the Sustain (or Damper) Pedal with your foot, all of the Dampers are moved away from the strings, so even if you release the keys while the pedal is depressed, the strings will continue to vibrate and produce sound. When the pedal is released, the Dampers return to their resting position, and the strings stop vibrating and the sound stops.

Using the Sustain Pedal

The Sustain Pedal is operated with the right foot. When using the pedal, your right heel should be placed firmly on the floor. The operation of the pedal itself should be silent. Avoid letting your foot "slap" the pedal and avoid letting the pedal "bump" when you release it. The Sustain Pedal has two main functions:

1. It is used to connect different chords to make them Legato so that there is no separation between them.
2. It is used to sustain notes belonging to the same chord, perhaps a broken chord or notes too far apart.

The Sustain Pedal Mark

℘ed. - Engage (depress) the Sustain Pedal   ✷ - Release the Sustain Pedal

When the Release symbol is immediately followed by the Engage symbol, this means to quickly "Change" the pedal. The pedal is Changed by quickly releasing and re-depressing the pedal, *at the moment and on the beat of the next note or chord above the the new "Engage Pedal" mark*. Take a look at the example below.

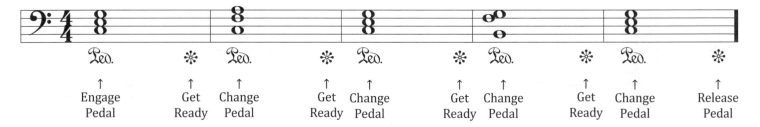

Practicing with the Sustain Pedal

Playing Legato Chords

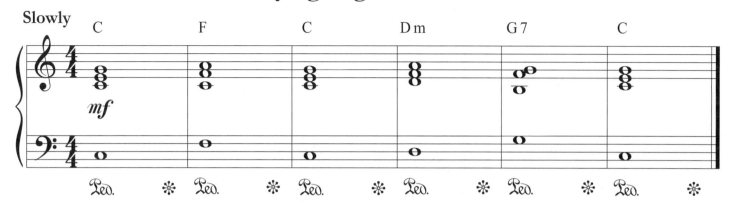

Connecting Chords which are Far Apart

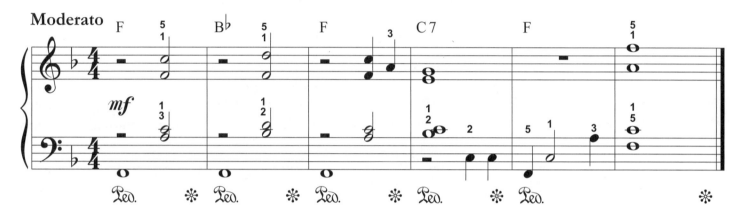

Connecting Broken Chords

CD Track 34

Major and Minor Thirds

We've learned that Intervals are measured by the number of letter names between the notes, and to calculate the size of an Interval, we count the number of letter names including the notes themselves. Using this formula, we can see that the distance between the notes C and E would be an Interval of a 3rd, and the distance between D and F would also be a 3rd. These two Intervals, while both 3rds, are quite different.

Counting up by half-steps, we can see that the distance from C to E is four half-steps, while the distance from D to F is only three half-steps. Both of the Intervals are thirds, but they are different types of thirds.

The Interval of a 3rd containing four half-steps is called a MAJOR THIRD
The Interval of a 3rd containing three half-steps is called a MINOR THIRD

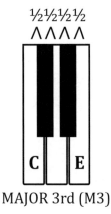

MAJOR 3rd (M3)

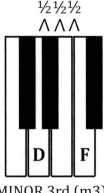

MINOR 3rd (m3)

Play the following scale written in Thirds, while listening to the difference between the Major and Minor 3rds.

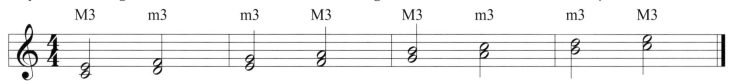

To convert a Minor 3rd to a Major 3rd, we must make the Interval one half-step larger.
One way to do this is to add a sharp to the top note.

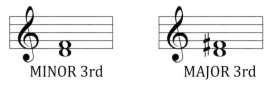

MINOR 3rd   MAJOR 3rd

Now, play the same scale with all of the Minor 3rds converted to Major 3rds. Listen to the difference.

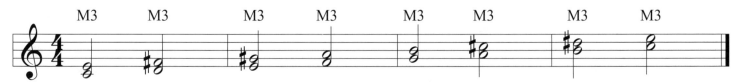

To convert a Major 3rd to a Minor 3rd, we must make the Interval one half-step smaller.
One way to do this is to add a flat to the top note.

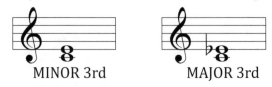

MINOR 3rd   MAJOR 3rd

And finally, play the same scale converted to all Minor 3rds, while you listen carefully to the Intervals.

You can see that it is easy to hear the difference between the Major 3rd and the Minor 3rd.

Rock Style

ROCK STYLE is characterized by the accent given to the normally unaccented 2nd and 4th beats by drummers and rhythm guitar players. Another characteristic of this style is the use of syncopation in the melody line. While the harmony (the chords) will typically still change on the first or third beats, the accented 2nd and 4th beats (also called the BACKBEATS) creates a "call and response" effect between the harmony and the rhythm. Rock Style evolved over the years from its early beginnings in the 1950s through the decades which followed into many different styles and combinations of styles, including Funk, Rhythm & Blues and Jazz Rock.

Classic 1950s Rock Style

Mid 1960s Rock Style

Did you know? The term JAZZ FUSION originated in the late 1960s from a combination of Rock and Jazz Styles.

The Blues

The BLUES is a musical form originating from the African American Spirituals of the late 19th Century. In its purest form, the Blues is based on a twelve measure, or TWELVE BAR, progression of chords in a strict pattern. Though the Blues has developed over the years into more complex variations, the original Twelve Bar structure remains the basic foundation of the Blues upon which all other modifications are based.

The Blues Chord Progression

The basic Blues Progression uses just three chords:

The I Chord (Tonic Chord) based on the 1st Degree of the Scale

The IV Chord (Sub-dominant Chord) based on the 4th Degree of the Scale

The V Chord (Dominant Chord) based on the 5th Degree of the Scale (V7 Chord also used)

The Basic Twelve Bar Structure of the Blues Chord Progression

The Slashes in the measures are called SLASH NOTATION. They are there to show each beat.
The important thing in the example below is the Chord Progression and number of measures for each chord.

Feelin' Blue

Jonathon Robbins

The Coda

The word CODA is from the Italian for "tail." It refers to a closing section of a piece. It may be as simple as a few measures or as complex as an entire section. In either case, it brings the piece to a conclusion. The Coda is usually annotated with the symbol, "⊕." D.C. and D.S. Repeats may be used with the Coda incorporated.

D.C. al Coda & D.S al Coda

You're familiar with both D.C al Fine and D.S. al Fine repeats. Coda Repeats work very much the same way. When you reach the measure with either "D.C. al Coda" or "D.S. al Coda" return to the appropriate place, as usual (the beginning for D.C. or the Segno for D.S.). The difference is, when you reach the end of the measure marked, "To Coda ⊕" skip directly to the Coda, which is marked, "⊕ Coda." Be sure not to jump to the Coda the first time through. You must first repeat the section, then jump to the Coda the second time.

Lazy Blues
CD Track 35

Jonathon Robbins

- 81 -

More About 6/8 Time

We've discussed that in 6/8 Time, while there are 6 beats per measure, there is actually a strong feeling of just two beats per measure. We also talked about the Imaginary Barline between beats 3 and 4 dividing the measure into two. Because of the 2 beats per measure "feel," eighth notes are typically beamed in groups of three. When two eighth notes appear with an eight rest in between, it is correct notation to beam the notes together to make it a little eaiser to read. Take a look below and see how easy this pattern is to read.

CORRECT NOTATION   INCORRECT NOTATION

Carnival of Venice
CD Track 36

Moderately   Traditional Italian

The Rhumba Rhythm

The RHUMBA ia a popular ballroom dance which originated in Cuba. People of African decent originally used the word as a synonym for "party." The Rhumba eventually evolved into a defined Cuban musical genre and dance form. The Rhumba rhythmn is characterized by syncopated accent pattern, as follows:

Beats: 1   &   2   &   3   &   4   &
Accents: >   >   >

Here's a Mexican classic with a traditional Rhumba rhythm in the left hand.

La Cucaracha

Mexican Folk Song

The Medley

Here's a fun MEDLEY of more Latin dance rhythms. A Medley is group of pieces strung together. It is meant to be performed as one complete piece. At the end of each section, the tune will have a clear ending, then a SEGUE (pronounced, "Seg-way"), which is a smooth transition to the next section in the Medley.

In the Medley below, be sure to notice the changes in the Key Signature as you transition to each new section.

Latin Dance Medley

The Samba

The Tango

The Cha-Cha

Types of Triads

Now that you have an understanding about Major and Minor Thirds, and the basic concept of the Triad, it's time to expand our discussion and look at the various combinations of Thirds and how they are combined to create four different types of Triad. As you know, a Triad is constructed by placing a Third on top of another Third, but since there are two different types of Thirds, this makes four ways which they can be combined.

The MAJOR TRIAD = Major 3rd with a Minor 3rd on top.

The MINOR TRIAD = Minor 3rd with a Major 3rd on top.

The AUGMENTED TRIAD = Major 3rd with a Major 3rd on top.

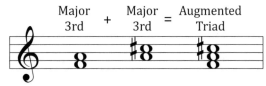

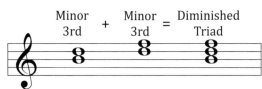

The DIMINISHED TRIAD = Minor 3rd with a Minor 3rd on top.

Chord Symbols

We've been using CHORD SYMBOLS throughout this book, but we should mention a few things about standard notation practices when it comes to Chord Symbols. The first thing you'll see is the Root of the Chord (the name of the Chord) with a capital letter, which may be followed by an accidental (as in B♭ or F♯).

After the Root of the Chord, you may see a lowercase letter (or letters), a symbol, or a number (in the case of seventh chord). Right now, we're going to concentrate on Triads, so here are the possible fully constructed Chord Symbols. There may be more than one way to notate a chord, but these are the most common:

C	D m or D min	F aug or F+	B dim
Major Chord	Minor Chord	Augmented Chord	Diminished Chord

Triads Built on the Notes of the C Major Scale

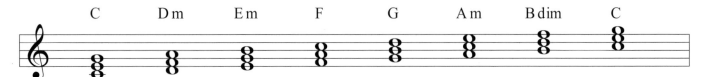

Broken Triads

Arpeggios

An ARPEGGIO is a type of Broken Chord. The word comes from the Italian word, "Arpeggiare," which means "to play the harp." Generally, the chords of an Arpeggio are played either up or down in succession. Proficiency at playing both Scales and Arpeggios provides a solid foundation for piants of all levels.

Swinging
CD Track 37

Ragtime

RAGTIME was a popular music genre which was very popular at the end of the 19th century and the early part of the 20th century. It is characterized by syncopated, or "ragged" rhythms. The African-American entertainer, Ernest Hogan was said to have pioneered the style, and is credited for coining the term, Ragtime, however, it is Scott Joplin who is by far the most remembered composer of this popular musical style. His piece, **The Entertainer (A Ragtime Two-Step)** is perhaps one of his best known works for the piano.

HINT: There's a D.S. al Coda Repeat. The Coda is just one measure. Look for it at the end.

The Entertainer
(A Ragtime Two-Step)
CD Track 38

Scott Joplin

The Relative Minor

Until now, you've seen a number of Key Signatures and have learned how to identify the Major Key which is indicated by that Key Signature. All Key Signatures, however, have two possible keys, the Major Key and its RELATIVE MINOR. A Relative Minor is a scale or key which has the same Key Signature as its RELATIVE MAJOR. The difference is the starting note or Tonic Note of the scale. For instance, we know that the Key of C Major has no sharps or flats, and the scale begins on the note, C. The Relative Minor of C Major is the Key of A Minor, and that scale, as you might have guessed, begins on the note, A. Is there a formula to figure this out?

YES ... There is.

To find the Relative Minor of any Major Key, go to the sixth note (or, Sixth Degree) of the scale. That is the starting note for the Relative Minor of that Key. The Minor Scale has same Key Signature, so it looks like this:

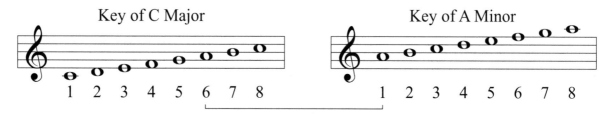

So, starting with the C Major Scale, if we go to the Sixth Degree of that scale (the note, A) and play a new scale starting on that note, we have the Relative Minor of C Major, the Key of A Minor, with the same Key Signature. Minor Keys tend to have what many people describe as a darker feeling, or perhaps a more somber tone.

Types of Minor Scales

The A Minor Scale you see above is in the form of what is called, the NATURAL MINOR, which is the Minor Scale played according to the Key Signature. If you play it, you can see that it sounds fine, but a little strange if you've been used to mostly Major Keys. The Natural Minor is rarely used in composition, but there are two other forms that are generally used. These other two forms are created by altering one or two tones in the Natural Minor Scale. The MELODIC MINOR SCALE is the more complicated one. It was originally created to accomodate the human voice. Let's skip that one, for now. The HARMONIC MINOR SCALE alters just one note. This scale provides a very pleasing transition, or CADENCE, from the V Chord back to the I Chord. The Harmonic Minor Scale is constructed by raising (or sharping) the seventh note (Degree) of the Minor Scale:

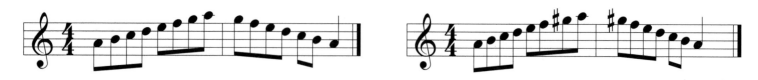

If you play both of these scales, we think you would agree that the second one, the Harmonic Minor, sounds much more interesting and you could even say more pleasing to the ear. There's a reason for this. That sharped seventh degree becomes a very important note in the V Chord of the Key. This may be a little advanced, so if you're interested, read on, and if not, we'll boil it down in the end.

The same rules apply in Minor Keys as far as the Tonic, Sub-dominant, and Dominant Chords are concerned (The I Chord, IV Chord, and V Chord). In the Key of A Minor, the Dominant (V) Chord would be E. A common Chord Progression is one that ends in V-I. You've seen it many times. Without that sharped seventh degree, in this case, G-sharp, our V Chord would be a Minor Triad, but when it's sharped, it becomes a Major Triad. Having a Major V or V7 Chord leading back to the Tonic Chord, in either a Major or Minor Key, is one of the most recognizable Cadences, and also one that is the most pleasing and satisfying to the ear.

That was the long explanation. The bottom line is that the Harmonic Minor creates a very pleasing transition from the V Chord back to the I Chord. We'll be concentrating on this form, for now, as in the following piece.

Playing the Harmonic Minor Form

The following tune, written during the Civil War, uses the Harmonic Minor form in the left hand chord harmonies. By the way, there is no marking that determines this. Pieces are written in a Key, in this case, the Key of A Minor. It is the altered notes that gives you an indication as to the form of the minor. This does not mean that the piece cannot contain other altered notes, but if you take a look at each occurance of the V Chord (the E7 Chord), you'll see the note, G-sharp, which is the sharped seventh degree of the A Minor Scale.

When Johnny Comes Marching Home

CD Track 39

The Sixteenth Note

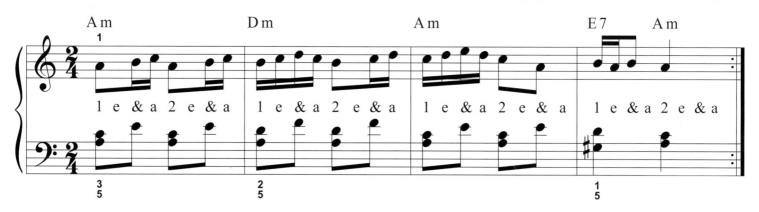

This is a
Sixteenth Note

Two Beamed
Sixteenth Notes

This is a
Sixteenth Rest

Two Sixteenth Notes
Equal One Eighth Note

Four Sixteenth Notes
Equal One Quarter Note

In 2/4, 3/4, or 4/4 Time, the Sixteenth Note receives One-Quarter Beat. Count the beat divisions like this:

1 e & a 2 e & a 3 e & a 4 e & a

Now, try this short exercise in 2/4 Time. Count the beats and be sure to play the Sixteenth Notes evenly.

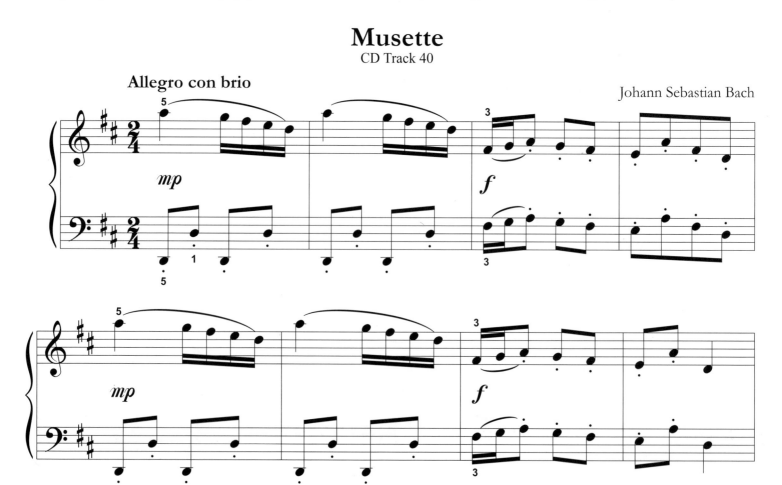

This next piece, by Johann Sebastian Bach, is also a selection from the Notebook for Anna Magdalena Bach. Aside from the many sixteenth note rhythms, you'll find that you will have to change hand positions frequently. Also, be sure to pay particular attention to the phrasing, staccato markings, and the dynamics.

Musette
CD Track 40

Allegro con brio

Johann Sebastian Bach

The Dotted Eighth Note

The DOTTED EIGHTH NOTE is just like any other dotted note. We could do the math, and figure out that in 4/4 Time, since the Eighth Note recieves one-half beat, then the Dotted Eight Note would receive three-quarters of a beat. Although that's accurate, there's a much easier way to think of dotted notes, especially when they are followed by a note of smaller duration. Let's look at beat sub-divisions, instead:

The examples above are all very similar. Even though some of the note values are different in each example, the second note is one-fourth of the total number of beats in the two note pattern. This is a much easier way to think about these types of dotted rhythms. Before long, this rhythm will become second nature and you'll soon have an imprint of this pattern without having to perform any complicated calculations. Dotted Rhythms of this type have the same rhythmic "feel" which you'll soon begin to recognize on sight.

Dotted Eighth - Sixteenth Note Exercise

Silent Night

Wolfgang Amadeus Mozart

A child prodigy from Salzburg, Wolfgang Amadeus Mozart composed at the age of five, performed for European Royalty, and composed for the Salzburg Court at age 17. After travelling to Vienna in 1781, he remained there for the remainder of his short life, and composed many of his most-loved symphonies, concertos, and operas. Mozart composed over 600 works, including the well-known opera, "Don Giovanni."

Minuet
(from the Opera, "Don Giovanni")

Wolfgang Amadeus Mozart

Modulation

MODULATION is the process of changing from one Key to another. There are many different types of modulation which define the process of changing keys. When a piece Modulates, you may see a new Key Signature, or simply accidentals on some of the notes. Right now, we'll just concentrate on what is known as DIRECT or STATIC MODULATION, where the piece changes key without a transitional chord progression.

The following piece Modulates from the Key of C Major, to G Major, then back to C Major. Notice the changes in the Key Signature when the modulation occurs. The Natural Sign in the Key Signature at the second Modulation cancels out the F-sharp in the previous Key. Also, notice the unique Cadence at the end.

Tumbling

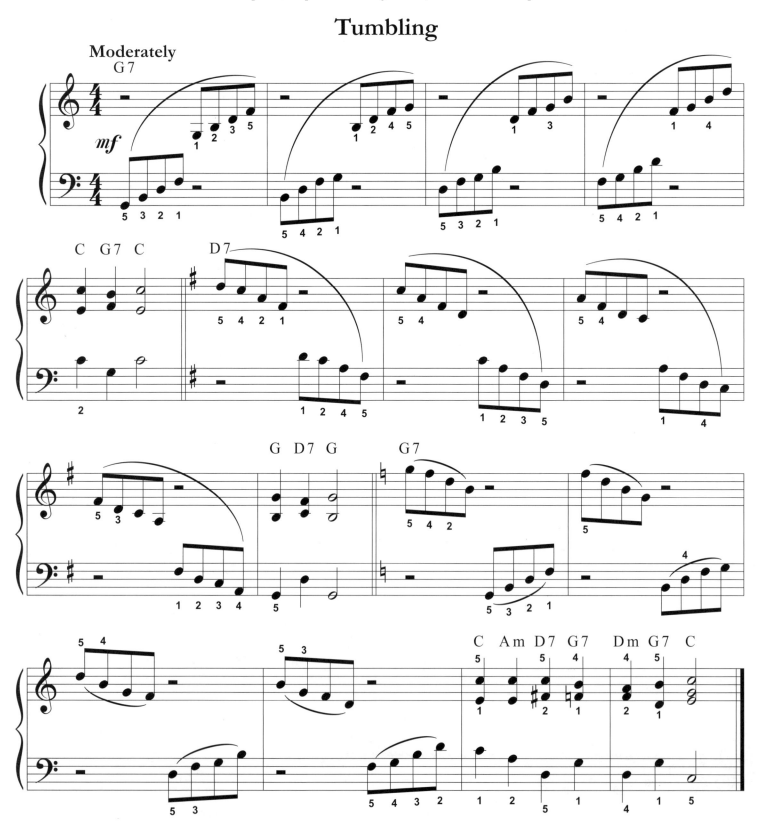

Counting 6/8 Time in "Two"

At faster Tempos, it's very difficult to count all six beats for pieces written in 6/8 Time. The 6/8 Time Signature does imply a strong feeling of just two beats per measure. This is even more apparent at a quicker Tempo. The note values, however, remain the same, since it is still 6/8 Time, but when you're counting in "Two," the Dotted Quarter Note appears to receive one beat, while the familiar group of three Eighth Notes feel more like an Eighth Note Triplet as you might see in other Time Signatures.

Tarantella is the name for a group of traditional Italian dances, usually written in 6/8 Time and characterized by fast, upbeat tempos. The title is often used generically, but actual dance names do vary by region.

Tarantella
CD Track 42

Advanced Syncopation

Syncopation is definately one of those things that you really can't practice too much. As you reach the end this course, you'll more than likely want to move on to play many types of music. You might be interested in more advance Classical works, perhaps original Ragtime or Popular Standards, or maybe even Jazz. You'll encounter Syncopated melodies in many of these styles, but when it comes to Syncopation, we always think of Scott Joplin and his many Ragtime classics. Here's an arrangement of **Maple Leaf Rag**, one of his best!

Maple Leaf Rag

CD Track 43

Scott Joplin

Common Major Scales

Common Harmonic Minor Scales

A Minor - Relative Minor of C Major

E Minor - Relative Minor of G Major

B Minor - Relative Minor of D Major

D Minor - Relative Minor of F Major

G Minor - Relative Minor of B♭ Major

C Minor - Relative Minor of E♭ Major

Arpeggio & Chord Reference Guide

(Common Major Keys)

Arpeggio & Chord Reference Guide

(Common Minor Keys)

A Minor - Relative Minor of C Major

E Minor - Relative Minor of G Major

B Minor - Relative Minor of D Major

D Minor - Relative Minor of F Major

G Minor - Relative Minor of B♭ Major

C Minor - Relative Minor of E♭ Major

Ethnic Favorites for Easy Piano
from Santorella Publications

Irish Favorites for Easy Piano

__TS121

ALL LYRICS
IN ENGLISH

Danny Boy • Kerry Dance • The Galway Piper
Cockles and Mussels • Irish Eyes Are Smiling
Come Back to Erin • The Irish Washerwoman
Sweet Rosie O'Grady • Tourelay and more.

Italian Favorites for Easy Piano

__TS122

ALL LYRICS
IN ITALIAN
& ENGLISH

Funiculi - Funicula • O Sole Mio • Ah! Mari!
Torna A Sorrento • Addio A Napoli • Tarantella
Santa Lucia • Serenade • Carnival of Venice
La Donna E'Mobile • Marcia Reale and more.

German Favorites for Easy Piano

__TS123

ALL LYRICS
IN GERMAN

Von Meinem Bergli Muß Ich Scheiden • Drei
Lilien Ö Freut Euch Des Lebens • Ein Prosit
Der Gemütlichkeit • Schwarzbraun Ist Die
Haselnuß • Heidschi Bumbeidschi and more…

Jewish Favorites for Easy Piano

__TS124

ALL LYRICS
IN HEBREW

Hava Nagila • Adir Hu • Adon Olam • Hatikva
Avinu Malkenu • Ayri Kaylohaynu • Daiyenu
Bahar Bagai • Eliyahu Hanavi • Chag Purim
Shalom Aleychem • Oy Hanukkah and more…

Polish Favorites for Easy Piano

__TS125

ALL LYRICS
IN POLISH
& ENGLISH

Annie Did It Wrong • Circus Polka • America
Coal Miner's Polka • The Blonde Bombshell
Who Stole the Keeshka? • Boom Chick-Chick
Anniversary Waltz • Bridal Chorus and more…

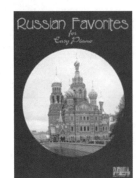

Russian Favorites for Easy Piano

__TS126

ALL LYRICS
IN RUSSIAN

Song of the Volga Boatmen (Ey Oochnyem!)
Dark Eyes • Kaleenka • Farewell (Proshtchai)
I Sing No More • Oh, Console Me! (Pozhaliey!)
Ach Zatchem Eta Notch • Bublitchki and more.

Greek Favorites for Easy Piano

__TS127

ALL LYRICS
IN GREEK

Saranta Palikaria • O Menussis • Susta Kritis
Su Ipa Mana M' Pantrepse Me • Samiotissa
Me Tis Elies • Makedonia Ksakusti • Karaguna
Rovas Kotsari • Thalassaki Mou and more…

French Favorites for Easy Piano

__TS128

ALL LYRICS
IN FRENCH

Ah! Vous Dirai-Je, Maman • Frère Jacques
Au Claire de la Lune • Fais Dodo • Farandole
Gymnopedie • La Marseilles • Skater's Waltz
O Canada • Vive la Compagnie and more…

Latin Favorites for Easy Piano

__TS166

ALL LYRICS
IN SPANISH

Adios Muchachos • Cielito Lindo • El Choclo
Cose, Cose, Cose • El Relicario • Estrellita
La Cumparsita • La Cucaracha • La Paloma
Rico Vacilon • La Golondrina and more…

SANTORELLA PUBLICATIONS
Post Office Box 60 • Danvers, MA 01923
info@santopub.com • www.santopub.com